TEXAS
BARBECUE

A guide to the best pits, products,
and prize-winning recipes in the Lone Star state

PARIS PERMENTER & JOHN BIGLEY

Also by Paris Permenter and John Bigley:
Day Trips from San Antonio and Austin (Two Lane Press)

First printing May 1994

ISBN: 0-925175-20-X

Printed in the United States of America

Text and cover designer: Jim Langford
Editor: Jane Doyle Guthrie

10 9 8 7 6 5 4 3 2 1 94 95 96 97 98

For corporate sales and special orders, or to receive a catalog, contact the publisher:

Pig Out Publications, Inc.
4245 Walnut Street
Kansas City, Missouri 64111
(816) 531-3119
(816) 531-6113 (fax)

CONTENTS

ACKNOWLEDGMENTS

How does one go about writing a guidebook to barbecue in Texas? Not without help.

The task before us was immense: Go forth and eat. We confined ourselves to that hotbed of barbecue activity, the Barbecue Belt, the region slicing through Central Texas and including the pits most people think of when they consider Texas barbecue. But since good eating knows no boundaries, we also strayed pretty far afield, hitting the pits in some of Texas's other most popular destinations as well.

No guide to Texas barbecue could be comprehensive. Our stomachs would not allow it. But we have tried to cover some of the best, places recommended by food writers, fellow travelers, town locals, chamber of commerce offices, and newspapers. In spite of our efforts, we've undoubtedly missed a few priceless pits, perhaps some of your own personal favorites. But perhaps that's part of the fun. No barbecue lover wants to think he has dined on the epitome of 'que. It's best to dream that perhaps the pinnacle of pork and the best of beef lie over the horizon, through a blue haze of smoke.

We took to the road as anonymous diners, walking into smoky joints and tony restaurants alike as two people just looking for a good dinner. We did not introduce ourselves to owners or employees; we just bellied up to the counter and ordered whatever sounded tasty. Often we called an establishment a few days later to verify a fact or two or to learn more about the history of the joint.

But we did not want to rely on our personal tastes alone, so we sought help. Frequently friends and family dutifully lent us their taste buds, dining with us and offering their opinions.

We must thank our own sausage taster, Lauren Bigley, who has cheerfully downed dozens of sausage wraps across the state. And Liz Bigley, who spent a busy July day with us searching for the best New Braunfels's pits had to offer.

Thanks also to Cara Bertron, who went out with us in search of San Antonio's finest. And to Lois Null, who led us through the pits of La Grange and Schulenburg. We sampled restaurants in the Big D thanks to Steve and Kathy Welch, who led us from the best known pits to some local favorites. In

Glen Rose, thanks to Gail Ramsey for helping us to find the best barbecue in the area. Out in El Paso, thanks go to Brad Cooper, who helped lead us to the tastiest 'que in West Texas.

We also must thank the folks who have introduced us to the barbecue world, helping us look beyond the plate and into the pit. Folks like Charlene Hahn of the Central Texas Barbecue Association and Jerry Burger of the North Texas Area Barbecue Cookers Association.

We are grateful also to the individuals and organizations who unselfishly shared with our readers their prize recipes, some of which have been carefully developed for years.

We'd like to thank Mom and Dad, a.k.a. Richard and Carlene Permenter, who tended our home pit and enabled us to travel and eat our way across Texas.

And, finally, thanks to the pitmasters who create art beside a smoking pit in 100-degree Texas heat. We've learned a lot from the people who have helped elevate Texas barbecue to national prominence.

INTRODUCTION

Barbecue is as much a symbol of Texas as the Lone Star and longhorns, or the two-step and the 10-gallon hat. At last count, Texas boasted over 1,300 barbecue joints, ranging from side-of-the-road greasehouses with slamming screen doors to sit-down restaurants with beautiful vistas, air conditioning, and even (gasp) wine lists. The business of BBQ rings up over a half-billion dollars annually, but more than that it's a cobweb of commerce that connects an otherwise diverse, sprawling state with a common mission: Go forth, Texans, and seek out good barbecue.

Throughout the Lone Star State, barbecue is everywhere. Whether it's at political functions, family reunions, or picnic lunches, barbecue brings folks together. When the PTA or the Lions Club needs a fundraiser, all turn to the pit. And when it comes to volunteer fire departments, small towns know that where there's smoke there's fire, hopefully from the pits used by local VFDs at their barbecue suppers.

Barbecue ranks with state politics in provoking heated discussion between Texans. One barbecue joint has a sign over its counter that says it best: "Bar-b-que, sex and death are subjects that provoke intense speculation in most Texans. Out of the three, probably bar-b-que is taken most seriously."

You'll find that's true when you ask any Texan his favorite smokehouse or, heaven forbid, you ask a pit owner for his barbecue recipe. The smoky meats are cooked according to secret methods that many pitmasters plan to take to their graves, but most recipes call for slow cooking over oak, hickory, pecan, or mesquite chips. The meat is rubbed with dry spices and finished off with a tomato-based sauce that can range from sweet to spicy.

One thing on which most Texans will agree is that barbecuing is not grilling. Grilling may be good, but to be labeled barbecue the meat must be cooked in a closed contraption to hold in the smoke that imparts its flavor on the chosen meat selection. Grilling is done in the open where the smoke dissipates before becoming an integral part of the meal itself. Grilling is also accomplished quickly, while barbecuing takes plenty of time, sometimes an entire (24-hour) day.

Beef rules most of the Texas barbecue pits in the form of brisket, ribs, sausage, and chopped beef. You'll also find plenty of chicken and pork, plus an occasional offering of mutton in East Texas and cabrito in West Texas. Nonetheless, beef is on every barbecue menu from Stubbs's in Lubbock to Sam's in Austin to Kreuz Market in Lockhart.

There are some terms to become familiar with in order to "parlez 'que" like a Texan:

BABY BACK RIBS—Ribs from a young hog; usually the most tender of the rib cuts.

BARBACOA—The Spanish took the Indian word *barbacoa* to describe this smoky meat, the basis for our own word barbecue. You will find barbacoa on the menu in many South Texas restaurants, especially Tex-Mex. It refers to a special type of barbecue: the head of a cow wrapped in cheesecloth and burlap, slow smoked in a pit.

BEEF CLOD—Part of the shoulder or the neck near the shoulder; used like brisket.

BRISKET—Chest muscle of a cow. This typically tough cut requires a long, slow cooking period to break down the fibrous meat. When many Texans say they're eating barbecue, they mean brisket. Every joint probably serves up this barbecue dish of Texas.

CABRITO—Young goat.

COUNTRY-STYLE PORK RIBS—Backbone of a hog. These ribs contain large chunks of meat and sometimes resemble a pork chop.

MARINADE—A seasoned liquid mixture in which meat is soaked prior to cooking. Acidic marinades such as those containing lime juice help tenderize meat. (*Note:* Acidic marinades should never be used in aluminum containers.)

RUB—Dry ingredients rubbed onto meat to season it during cooking.

SAUCE—The flavored liquid used as a condiment after the meat has cooked. In Texas, most sauces are tomato-based.

SKIRT STEAK—Diaphragm muscle of a cow. This tough cut is usually used for fajitas after marinating.

SLAB OF RIBS—A whole side of the rib cage.

SMOKE RING—The telltale pink ring in meat that authenticates it as barbecue.

SOP—A basting sauce applied during the barbecuing process.

SPARERIBS—The lower portion of a hog's ribs.

TEXAS HIBACHI—A used 55-gallon drum used as a barbecue cooker.

One thing that's no secret is that the best barbecue joints (restaurants may be too fine a word) are the ones that usually look the worst. Walls streaked by smoke? Menu just a sign on the wall? Food served on butcher paper with a side order of cheap white bread or soda crackers? Congratulations, you've found a real Texas barbecue pit. Roll up your shirt sleeves and get to work.

It just doesn't get any better than this.

PART ONE
ALONG THE BARBECUE BELT

You've heard of the Bible Belt and the Sun Belt. Welcome to the Barbecue Belt. This strip of Texas is what usually comes to mind when folks mention Texas barbecue. This is the land of barbecue shrines like Elgin's Southside Market, Taylor's Louis Mueller's, Llano's Cooper's Pit, and Lockhart's Kreuz Market. This is Mecca for meat lovers, the Promised Land for porcine aficionados, the Shangri-la of smoke. This is Central Texas, the region that stretches from Llano to the west to Schulenburg to the east. It cuts a smoky swath through the hill country, taking in the capital city of Austin, the Alamo city of San Antonio, and countless small communities where the barbecue joint is the most happening place in town.

Unlike other barbecue hot spots like Kansas City and Memphis, Texas has no capital of 'que. Instead it's a title shared throughout this Barbecue Belt region. Most places in this area share a similar cooking style, serve up their plates with sides of pinto beans, coleslaw, potato salad, and white bread, and offer squirt bottles of tomatoey barbecue sauce on every table. They also offer you a chance to eat with small-town Texans, from bankers to bricklayers, who frequent these little joints every day at noon.

Barbecue got its start in this region in the meat markets and butcher shops. These pioneer merchants were determined to find a use for cuts that weren't selling. On the weekends, they began smoking those quickly aging meats, hoping to make them more palatable with an infusion of smoke. It worked. Like a gaseous billboard, the smell of barbecue soon permeated the small towns and captured the attention of those doing their Saturday marketing. Farmers and ranchers in town for weekend trading came by the meat market and found an inexpensive lunch served up on the only plate a butcher had on hand: butcher paper.

Eventually, farm and ranch families began making the meat market a regular weekend stop, dining off the back of their wagons. Soon some meat markets began to put up a few picnic tables for customers. Today the best joints still have a picnic table or two. Some still serve their product on butcher paper. And in all but a few cases, the meal is still inexpensive.

RESTAURANT LISTING

AUSTIN

Word has it that the site for the capital of Texas was chosen while the President of the Republic of Texas was hunting buffalo. Mirabeau B. Lamar came across a community named Waterloo, and, entranced by the rolling hills, he selected this spot as the new capital city and renamed it Austin. But maybe the real reason he chose the site was the readily available oak, mesquite, and pecan wood. Lamar probably knew a barbecue hot spot when he saw one.

Today, Central Texas is the capital of barbecue in the Lone Star State, at last count dotted with over 80 'que restaurants. You'll find smokehouses of every size and shape in Austin, from traditional barbecue joints to one with a slight Hawaiian flavor.

ANTONE'S BILLY BLUES
Colorado & W. Second Sts.

Cash/credit. Table service.

Since 1975, Clifford Antone has been drawing music lovers to Austin with top-name blues acts in his club, Antone's. But as his popularity increased, the crowds grew. Antone's was just too small for nationally known road acts.

But then along came Billy Blues, the San Antonio–based chain of barbecue restaurants. Clifford Antone and Peter Gallagher, founder of Billy Blues, joined together to bring Austin the best of two worlds: blues and barbecue. Billy Blues has known the value of this combination since the chain began in 1990, but will elevate the concept to a new scale with this upcoming restaurant. Antone's Billy Blues, all 21,000 square feet of it, will be housed in a former plastics factory that recently underwent a million dollars' worth of renovation to make it the capitol of the capital city's live music scene. Two performance areas will accommodate both small acts and road shows, plus the restaurant will serve up what Billy Blues makes best: barbecue.

For more on the Billy Blues offerings, see the review later in this section of the San Antonio restaurant that started this chain.

ARTZ RIB HOUSE
2330 S. Lamar. (512) 442-8283

Cash/credit. Table service/take out. Catering.

Ask Austin barbecue lovers what they love about Artz's, and they'll come up with an immediate answer: ribs. This is Rib Land, the place where all your dreams about ribs can come true. Whether your wish is pork or beef ribs, Artz's holds the magic wand, or in this case, the rib bone, to make it all appear before you. Pork lovers can choose from country-style pork ribs, cut to resemble pork chops, or tender baby back ribs. They're both winners. You can also select the beef rib plate, overflowing with three large ribs.

Can't decide? Pick the combination plate for your favorite two out of three. We were especially impressed with the baby back ribs, cooked until the meat was tender enough to suck off the bone. They're served with a side of sauce that's not spicy enough to overtake the rib flavor, but flavorful enough to know you're adding some wonderful smoky taste to an already perfect rib.

If you're looking for something other than ribs, check out the menu for brisket (1/3-pound servings on the plates), smoked chicken, sausage (Austin's own Smoky Denmarks), and skewered chargrilled shrimp. The plates all come with spicy potato salad, crispy coleslaw, and pinto beans, plus pickles, onion slices, and bread.

Artz's has a large, sparsely decorated dining room, but if the weather's nice, head outside. Here you can hear nightly live music ranging from country to blues from either a screened porch or the open air patio.

BB SMOKEHOUSE
8664 Spicewood Springs Rd. (512) 258-3063
Cash / credit. Order / pick up. Catering.

We had to know the truth. What did the "BB" in BB Smokehouse mean? Bountiful barbecue? Beautiful brisket? Bodacious beans? Like good journalists, we sought out the answers. We ate the barbecue. We devoured the brisket. We feasted upon the beans. And the answer? It could have been any of our earlier guesses. The plates were heaped with barbecue and beans, all of it excellent. But our theories were all wrong.

BB is Bruce Bainter. Like any proud pitmaster, Bruce named his smokehouse for himself. And he has good reason to be proud.

Order one of the plates; it includes a huge helping of meat plus three side dishes. We opted for a three-meat platter with pork ribs, lean brisket, and sausage. The brisket was trimmed of fat and full of smoky taste. The pork ribs were tender, meaty, and so good we found ourselves sucking on the bones to extract just one more taste from each one. And the spicy sausage was some of Elgin's best. On your plates, you can also order chicken, chopped beef, or ham, all served with a light orange, almost caramel-colored sauce that's slightly syrupy and sweetish. It's a little different from the usual tomatoey sauces found in most Central Texas pits, but we found it a perfect complement to the meat.

Bruce has a whole list of side dishes you can select, including pintos, black-eyed peas, coleslaw, potato salad, sweet cornbread, a mini ear of corn, chips, jalapeños, or a mini wheat loaf. The potato salad, a mayonnaise-based creation, has chunks of potato interspersed with finely chopped pickles and red peppers. If you don't mind having only two side dishes instead of three, you can have a baked potato. (Bruce also serves a special Smokehouse Stuffed Potato, a wicked combination of baked potato with sour cream and butter stuffed with chopped beef and topped with barbecue sauce and cheese.)

If you're on the go at lunch, you can select a sandwich with any of Bruce's meats, or have a fajita. We returned to BB Smokehouse for lunch one day, telling ourselves we were doing research (really we couldn't get those fajitas out of our minds). The fajitas are an excellent quick lunch, filled with lean sliced beef or moist chicken. You can even order the fajita special, with two flour tortillas, extra lean brisket, beans, sour cream, cheese, and picante sauce. There's also a Frito pie made with chopped beef and beans, and in cold weather a version with chili.

Like its smoky product, the dining room at the BB Smokehouse is about as Texan as you can get. There's a collection of gimme caps behind the counter, which sports a collection of license plates from around the country. Barbed-wire art hangs on the wall, and the stereo plays gutbucket country and western music.

BEN'S LONG BRANCH BAR-B-Q
900 E. 11th St. (512) 477-2516

Cash/credit. Order/pick up. Catering.

Downtown workers and interstate highway travelers know Ben's. Just a half block off I-35, this smokin' joint is a barbecue capital. Owner Ben Wash serves up pork ribs, lean brisket, spicy sausage, mutton, and chicken with sides of beans and creamy potato salad.

Spend a few minutes reading the clippings that decorate the walls of Ben's. Stories that tell of charity benefits and celebrity diners, both recipients of Ben's goodwill and good cooking, dot the dining room.

We were especially fond of the brisket, served lean and without a trace of fat, and the pork ribs, blackened to testify to their trial by smoke. Memories of both these dishes will keep us coming back for more.

BRAGGERS BAR-B-Q
1519 W. Anderson Ln. (512) 452-4382

Cash/credit. Order/pick up. Catering.

Geraldine Harr is a woman in a man's world. The owner of Braggers Bar-B-Q, this entrepreneur realizes she's something of an oddity on the barbecue joint circuit. "There's not a lot of women in the business," she admits. Her years working a hot smoker go back a ways. Geraldine once worked for Tom Painter, a barbecue baron who owned restaurants in Longview and Kilgore. He originally owned this business under the name of Painter's Bar-B-Q Company. But after five years, Tom and wife Carol were ready to move on to other business interests and began looking around for someone to buy their north Austin pit. "I was in the right place at the right time," Geraldine explains. Before she knew it, Geraldine was purchasing the joint that had used many of her own recipes for years.

The brisket is one of Geraldine's best offerings. Smoked 18 hours over hickory, it is tender and lean. We enjoyed thinly sliced brisket without a touch of fat, served up with a side of spicy secret sauce. The beef ribs make a great second meat if you're looking for a full plate. Each rib weighs in at a hefty half pound, each smoked to bovine perfection. The ribs are dry, cooked with a rub and served with sauce on the side.

Sausage lovers will find Elgin's finest served here. The all-beef sausage is spicy and juicy, served either as plates or in that kids' favorite, the sausage wrap. With the plates, choose from beans, coleslaw, or potato salad. They're all made fresh daily.

Braggers sells sandwiches, too. Select a Sloppy Joe, made from brisket trimmings, or a chopped beef sandwich for an economical lunch.

Homemade pudding tops off the meal. A friendly "Don't Forget the Banana Pudding" sign reminds diners to order that barbecue restaurant favorite. Of course, with a homemade dessert like this one, made with bananas and vanilla wafers, no one needs any reminding.

Ask Geraldine what the specialty of Braggers Bar-B-Q is and she'll point out the friendly staff and the homey atmosphere. And that's no idle bragging.

BRANCH BBQ
1779 Wells Branch Pkwy. (512) 990-5282

Cash/credit cards. Order/pick up.

For years Charles and Carol Lange's friends tried to get them to open a barbecue restaurant in their Wells Branch neighborhood. For years the couple eyed the strip center across from their home, pondering a pit of their own. Finally they took the plunge, and it has paid off. Branch BBQ is as good as you can get. Sitting in the middle of Suburbia, you might pass up a strip center barbecue joint as just a yuppie eatery with sauce bottles on the table. But what you'll find here is barbecue as authentic as that served in any greasehouse.

Carol says there are three secrets to making barbecue special. First, knowing how to cook it. Second, knowing how to season it. Finally, giving it a little TLC. From the taste of Branch's smoky delights, this pit puts a lot of TLC in its work. Smoked with a combination of mesquite and oak, the brisket is juicy, the beef and pork ribs are fall-apart-in-your-hands tender, and the pork loin is flavorful and smoke filled. You can also choose from chicken or Elgin sausage. Plates come with a choice of two side dishes: potato salad, mashed potatoes and gravy, corn on the cob, coleslaw, or fried rice.

Fried rice? Yep, and that's what makes Branch BBQ a little different. "People are a lot more health-conscious now," explains Carol when asked about the rice on the menu. To offer an entree for those watching the cholesterol, Branch has some unique specialties: chicken or beef fried rice and smoked catfish. "People want fish that's not breaded or fried," says Carol. Calorie counters will even find a salad bar in this joint.

Of course, for those not watching their waistlines, there are temptations galore on the menu. That Texas favorite, Frito pie, even makes an appearance, but with a bow toward its barbecue surroundings. You can order this Lone Star delicacy with either chili or chopped beef topping.

Top off the meal with banana pudding, cheesecake, peach cobbler, or a selection of Texas's own Blue Bell ice cream.

COUNTY LINE ON THE LAKE
5404 RR 2222. (512) 346-3664
Cash/credit. Table service. Catering.

COUNTY LINE ON THE HILL
6500 W. Bee Caves Rd. (512) 327-1742
Cash/credit. Table service. Catering.

Walk in most Texas barbecue joints wearing a coat and tie and you'll be immediately branded a "city slicker." Well at the County Line, three-piece suits sit side by side with Wranglers and Levis. This is about as fancy as a barbecue restaurant gets, the kind of place where you might go to celebrate a special event with some special food. But don't think you're going to find a gussied-up menu here. No way. The menu, printed on "Little Chief" notepad reproductions, has the same offerings found at the smokiest, greasiest pit in the Lone Star State. (There's even white bread listed on the menu.)

But the real test of 'que quality is the product. Is this a citified version of a Texas classic? Is the meat meek and mild or can the diner tell it has been cooked, not in an oven, but in a smoky pit? Put your worries aside. The County Line, whichever location you choose, has the real thing. The meats are smoked for 18 to 20 hours daily, then trimmed of any fat. The result is as pure a barbecue as you'd find at a roadside stand.

The County Line on the Hill is the original restaurant in a chain that now includes eight locations in Texas plus others in Albuquerque, Denver, Oklahoma City, and Colorado Springs. This Bee Caves location is housed in a historic rock building with a 20-mile view of the hill country. Get a table on the stone patio if the weather complies.

The County Line on the Lake is set in an old lake lodge, right on the shores of Lake Austin. (Out on the lake all day and don't want to go home to get the car? No problem—just dock at the restaurant.)

There are plenty of reasons to go to the County Line restaurants, but the best ones are simple: beef ribs, baby backs, brisket, and sausage. We like to order country-style. Have your table order this all-you-can-eat extravaganza and you'll feast on beef ribs, brisket, and sausage served family style, with huge bowls of sour-cream potato salad, crunchy coleslaw, and tasty pintos. The side dishes are made from scratch daily. There's even homemade bread that rises twice before baking.

We couldn't pick a favorite meat among the country-style offerings. But why try? Just loosen your belt another notch and enjoy this Bacchanalian feast. If you've saved room—all right, you couldn't have saved room, but if you can stuff yourself even more, there's also hot fruit cobbler topped with homemade ice cream.

FIVE STAR SMOKEHOUSE
3638 Bee Caves Rd. (512) 328-1157

Cash / credit. Order / pick up. Catering.

Located in the hills west of town, this restaurant thrives on country atmosphere and good barbecue. Dine outside on the patio under the shade of tall oaks or indoors in a building full of rustic charm, complete with screen door and rough wood floors.

This restaurant boasts an extensive menu. Take your pick from brisket, baby back ribs, pork loin, smoked ham, smoked chicken, smoked turkey, and sausage. Our favorites were the tender brisket and the baby back ribs, a rosy red dusted with secret spices served with a side of sauce. The baby backs are slow-cooked over charcoal. The brisket, turkey, ham, pork shoulder, and sausage are slowly smoked 12 to 15 hours to reach barbecued bliss.

Plates are served with an excellent potato salad, beans, pickle, onion, and bread. There's also a long line of sandwiches to select from, including the plate meats plus pork shoulder, grilled cheese, and burgers. Specialties of the house are baked potato with barbecue and barbecue nachos—one of our favorites!

Save room for the home-baked pies—apple, chocolate, chocolate pecan, buttermilk, Toll House, and key lime—or a piece of old-fashioned peach cobbler.

THE GREEN MESQUITE BARBEQUE AND MORE
1400 Barton Springs Rd. (512) 479-0485
Cash / credit. Table service. Catering
13450 Research Blvd. (512) 335-9885
Cash / credit. Table service. Catering.
6155 Hwy. 290 in Oak Hill. (512) 892-0879
Cash / credit. Table service. Catering.

The most difficult part of dining at this joint is deciding what to eat: The menu is enormous for a smokehouse. In the plate section alone, you can select beef brisket, pork ribs, chicken, smoked turkey, sausage, ham, and combinations. Then there are the sandwiches, and the burgers, and the "and more" section, and . . .

But first things first. At the Green Mesquite, what comes first is barbecue. We tried the brisket, ribs, and sausage, and liked them all. The brisket was carved thin, trimmed of fat, and filled with plenty of smoky zest to attest to its slow cooking. The meaty and tender pork ribs would do any pig proud. And the sausage was spicy and tasty, with plenty of sauce on the side.

With the plates come side orders, again a bigger selection than you'd find in most joints. Spicy pinto beans, tangy coleslaw, and creamy potato salad are all here, plus corn on the cob and Cajun rice. If you've never had Cajun rice, here's a chance to enjoy a good representative sample—this is a jazzed-up, spiced-up version of an old standby. If someone in your group doesn't want barbecue, try a burger, taco basket, chef salad, chicken-fried steak, jambalaya, or the catfish plate.

The downtown Green Mesquite and the north location are both known for Friday, Saturday, and Sunday night music sessions featuring local talent. The Barton Springs location has an outdoor biergarten where you can dine at picnic tables and listen to some homemade blues. One thing's for certain, though. There's no reason to be blue after a visit to the Green Mesquite.

IRON WORKS
100 Red River. (512) 478-4855 or (800) 669-3602

Cash / credit card. Order / pick up / delivery.

When ironsmith Fortunat Weigl open his foundry at this spot in 1935, he probably never envisioned that one day Austin's movers and shakers would gather here for power lunches over plates of powerful barbecue. In those days, this was an ironworks shop, where the German immigrant and his sons Lee and Herbert produced handwrought decorative items. Their work was found in many stately homes in the city and also adorning the state capitol, the University of Texas, and Texas A&M.

In 1977 the ironworks closed its doors as a shop and was transformed into one of Austin's most popular downtown smokehouses. The building, complete with historic marker, is decorated with hundreds of brands, a reminder of its earlier life.

Today Iron Works is a rib bone's throw from the Austin Convention Center and just minutes from downtown offices and the state capitol. It's the spot for lunch on a warm spring day, when diners can sit at a picnic table on the outside deck, watch the turtles sun on the banks of Waller Creek, and wrap their hands around a rib fit for a king.

Iron Works' slogan is "Real Texas barbecue in a country atmosphere." Even though the ties outnumber the T-shirts on most days, this is an authentic smokehouse all right, from the brands on the walls to the squirt bottles and rolled paper towels that top each table. Whether your tastes run to beef, chicken, or sausage, Iron Works will make you happy. The ribs are cooked to smoky perfection, the brisket is tender, and the sausage (a combination of beef and pork) is spicy enough to send some diners back for an iced tea refill. To round out the plates, select from potato salad, coleslaw, or beans.

If you need to take a barbecue break, there's even Texas chili on the menu, with cold Lone Star beer to wash it down.

MOORE'S BAR-B-QUE
4412 Medical Pkwy. (512) 459-9388
Cash. Order/pick up. Catering.

Pamit Moore says that his barbecue business is kind of a hobby. As a senior equipment operator for the city of Austin, Pamit is a busy man, but he makes time to prepare barbecue. We should all be so lucky to have a hobby like Pamit's. Some people collect stamps, some collect books. You might say that Pamit collects art. The art of making some of the tastiest barbecue in Austin.

Pamit started out making barbecue for the city picnic every year, and one day he decided that this could become a business. "I kind of like doing what I'm doing, and people seem to like it," he says. So five years ago Pamit and his wife Gloria started Moore's Bar-B-Que in the medical district of town. It's located on a tiny triangle of land sandwiched between two streets. But that's OK. Pamit and Gloria still have plenty of room for their pit, a little restaurant, and some picnic tables. That's all their customers want. That and some tasty barbecue.

Taste is what the Moores say sets their product apart from other smokehouses. "We do have flavor," says Pamit. "That's what makes us different from the rest. We flavor our meats." A sign over the counter proclaims, "You've tried the rest, now eat at the best." And what's the best of the best? Pamit explains that their specialties are brisket, turkey, and chicken. You can also choose from sausage, pork, and beef ribs, Frito pie with barbecue, chopped beef sandwiches, or lunch specials like beef sausage on rice. They're served up with peppery pintos and a mustard-based potato salad that will have you reaching for the iced tea. Lovers of porcine specialties can even have cracklin. Finish off with pralines, blackberry or peach cobbler, or banana pudding.

If you attend the Travis County MHMR Rib Ticklin' Affair, you'll see Pamit and Gloria selling their spicy ribs. But don't wait for that annual event. Head down to Moore's. After one of these plates, you'll be wanting more of Moore's.

POK-E-JO'S SMOKEHOUSE
9828 Great Hills Trail. (512) 338-1990
Cash/credit cards. Order/pick up. Catering.

Fifteen years ago, a man named Porky and a man named Joe decided to open a barbecue joint in north Austin. Like pit owners around the country, they wanted to use their own monikers when it came time to christen the smoke-house. But would people eat at a place called Porky Joe's? So Pok-E-Jo's was born, raised for over a decade in a house off Burnet Road. Complete with horseshoe pits and volleyball courts, it became an Austin institution for families looking to do some barbecue dining.

But one day, the Mo-Pac expansion meant the relocation of many North Austin businesses, and the little house on Burnet Road was bulldozed. Pok-E-Jo's was without a home. The smokehouse headed north on Burnet Road, only to be relocated once again a few years later. But you can't keep a good barbecue pit down. Even though Pok-E-Jo's has been a restaurant on the move, its loyal customers have been glad to follow. Today Pok-E-Jo's has two homes, one in north Austin in the Great Hills center off US 183 and another in Round Rock off Interstate 35 (see the Round Rock section for location).

The Austin pit is a popular stop with businessmen for lunch and with moviegoers at night. Be ready to stand rib-to-rib to place your order on Saturday nights when the lines can be long and the wait can be, well, pokey. You'll see that it's time well spent as soon as you receive a plate heaped with a selection of lean meats and tasty side dishes.

Deciding to eat at Pok-E-Jo's is simple; the hard part lies in whether to order the smoky beef ribs the size of nightsticks, the tender pork ribs, the juicy brisket, or the mild or spicy sausage. There's even pork loin, chicken, ham, and sometimes turkey to make your decision that much tougher. Smoked 16 to 20 hours over green mesquite, every choice is a winner.

Give yourself a break and have a combination plate with two or three meats. The strength of those Styrofoam plates is put to the test with over a half pound of meat, Texas toast, and two side orders. Making the ordering process a little pokier for diners, there are seven side dishes: coleslaw, potato salad, corn on the cob, french fries, beans, fried okra, and even broccoli salad. All the side dishes are 100% fresh. We don't think you can go wrong with the crisp coleslaw and the chunky, mustard-tinged potato salad with kosher dill pickles.

The Pok-E-Jo's menu offers two types of sausage, both of which feature recipes specially prepared for the restaurant. The mild variety is produced in Fort Worth by a company that's been churning out sausage since the turn of the century. The all-beef sausage is made in Taylor, and it is a barbecue lover's delight, both peppery and spicy.

Cool the burn with some homemade banana pudding. The serving is generous enough to share—but who'd want to?

THE SALT LICK
See the description in the Driftwood section.

SAM'S BAR-B-CUE
2000 E. 12th St. (512) 478-0378
Cash. Order/pick-up.

Sam's is a smokin' place. In 1992, it was literally smoking—in fact, it was on fire. A kitchen inferno resulted in the closing of this classic Austin pit. But local citizens weren't about to let a favorite East Austin eatery go up in smoke. A volunteer group got together and rebuilt Sam's. Soon it rose like the mythical phoenix, and Austin once again boasted one of the finest barbecue joints on the planet.

Go to Sam's with a big appetite because you're going to get a big plate, one loaded down with meats and side dishes. We ordered plates of ribs and brisket and ran out of room long before we ran out of food. You can also choose from chicken, spicy sausage, and even mutton.

The side dishes are equally generous. The beans, fiery with lots of black pepper, are hot enough to make you grab for the iced tea and good enough to make you wonder how you ever enjoyed beans anywhere else. The potato salad helps cool the burn, and if that doesn't work, grab a slice of white bread.

There's a small dining room at Sam's decorated with newspaper clippings featuring Stevie Ray Vaughn. The late blues musician was a devoted Sam's customer, even making some long distance call-in orders for Sam's specialities when he was on the road. It's easy to see why.

It just doesn't get any better than this.

SMOKEY J'S BARBEQUE
7008 RR 620. (512) 331-4888
Cash. Order/pick up.
RR 1431 (west of Cedar Park). (512) 267-2706
Cash. Order/pick up.

If blood is thicker than water, then where does barbecue sauce fall? It must be pretty darn thick, at least in the case of friends like James Clift and Nancy and Ray Baumgart. James started the Smokey J's on RR 620 about 12 years ago. "He just came home one day and said he was going to give it a try," says James's wife. "He started out with a little cooker on the side of the road."

Well, James's product was so good that soon Smokey J's grew in size, and word of his pit spread. It started the Clifts' friends, Nancy and Ray, thinking about a pit of their own. About five years ago, they decided that they'd like to open a barbecue restaurant, too. Why not call it Smokey J's? Soon the Clifts were showing the Baumgarts how it was done. "They're friends of ours, and they showed us how to get ours going. We use the same kind of pit and same kind of wood," explains Nancy.

Mostly the offerings are the same at the two locations. Both specialize in brisket. "I think our specialty is the brisket because we serve it with no fat," says James. "We use really good brisket." James is right. Brisket sandwiches don't get any better that the ones from Smokey J's. We've eaten a mountain of brisket sandwiches, and these stand out as the king of the hill. The brisket is sliced paper thin with a deli meat cutter and piled over an inch high on white or wheat bread. There's not a tough spot in it.

But don't stop with the brisket sandwich. The sausage, Austin's own Smoky Denmarks, is spicy but not too greasy. If you're on the go, you can have a sausage wrap in bread, a winner with kids, or in a flour tortilla, our personal favorite. Smokey J's also has ham, fajitas, and chicken, plus the Baumgarts' RR 1431 location serves up ribs and plate lunches.

The location on RR 1431 has a small dining room, and the Ranch Road 620 joint has some picnic tables outside, although most of their business is carryout. Located on the way to Lake Travis, the 620 pit is a popular stop with picnickers looking to pick up some unbeatable barbecue. Thanks to the Clifts and the Baumgarts, diners can choose either location and come out winners. But after all, what are friends for?

SMOKY DENMARKS SAUSAGE CO.
3505 E. Fifth St. (512) 385-0718
Cash.

This is not a restaurant, but a place to buy Austin's most widely sold sausage. Smoky Denmarks sausage is known for its lack of grease, and it's served in many of the barbecue joints around Central Texas. Drop by the downtown Austin store and buy some for yourself. (It is not available by mail.) The store also sells smoked briskets (cooked or uncooked), hamburger patties, breakfast patties, and bacon.

BASTROP

Located southeast of Austin on TX 71, the small town of Bastrop is tucked deep in the Lost Pines. Bastrop is a popular day trip for Austinites looking for a country getaway and antique shopping.

BASTROP BBQ AND MEAT MARKET
919 Main St. (512) 321-7719

Cash. Order / pick up.

Barbecue began in the meat markets as a way to sell certain cuts of meat that customers just were not interested in taking home. Smart butchers started using the unsold cuts to make sausage, and they threw some of the tougher cuts over the fire to make them more palatable. Soon customers began coming by for the barbecue itself, served up on a sheet of rosy pink butcher paper.

So Bastrop BBQ and Meat Market has a fine tradition behind it. With one taste of their flavorful product, you'll see that they're doing their part to hold up that tradition. Bastrop is an excellent place to visit anyway, but even if Bastrop BBQ and Meat Market were the only place in town, it would still be worth the drive.

You can have the sausage, brisket, rib eye, or chicken served with a side of potato salad and beans, and you'll come out well fed and happy. Grab a table, sit back in the building that's over 100 years old, and imagine what barbecue was like when the meat market was also the barbecue restaurant. If it was anything like this, times must have been pretty good.

MR. BAR-B-QUE
TX 71 E. (512) 321-5281

Cash. Order / pick up. Catering.

Tucked beneath towering pines on busy TX 71, this little barbecue joint is nothin' fancy. The dining room is semi-dark, lit by the glow of a small television screen and filled with the conversation of local residents. Magazines are stacked high for diners who want to read as they chew on some brisket or sausage. There's even a shelf of used books for sale.

Or you could spend some time reading the menu, because it is long and the selections are many. Pick a plate with brisket, sausage, or ribs served with beans, potato salad, and slaw, or a sandwich, chopped or sliced beef or sausage. There's also Mexican food and catfish for those who need to take a break from the pits.

BLANCO

The little town of Blanco is located 51 miles north of San Antonio on US 281. It is nestled in the hill country, tucked between surrounding granite hills that are home to numerous ranches.

PHIL'S BBQ AND DELI
115 Main (US 281). (210) 833-2139

Cash. Order/pick up. Catering.

Phil Anderson opened this barbecue eatery in downtown Blanco several years ago. "This place started as a butcher shop," the pitmaster explains. "I took it over and turned it into a barbecue restaurant." Today the charming restaurant, with checked tablecloths and a homey small-town atmosphere, still hints at its butcher shop days. You place your order at a meat market counter stocked with numerous side dishes: pasta salad, cucumber salad, coleslaw, and chunky potato salad. All side dishes, like everything else at Phil's, are strictly homemade.

But as good as they are, the side dishes are just gravy. The real reason local residents come to Phil's is the meat: brisket, sausage, pork ribs, chicken, pork, turkey, and ham. Phil says his specialties are ribs, brisket, and turkey. We didn't have the chance to try the turkey, so we'll have to take Phil's word about that. We did order the ribs and brisket, and if the rest of the offerings are as good as these, then it's easy to see why Phil's is so popular with the locals. The pork ribs were tender and tasty, and the brisket was lean and moist, with a deep smoky flavor that made us wish we weren't sharing a plate.

BUCHANAN DAM

Buchanan Dam is situated, appropriately enough, next to the massive dam of Lake Buchanan, the largest of the Highland Lakes. The small fishing village is located on TX 29 northwest of Austin. During April, this town is abloom with bluebonnets, and visitors come from around the state to tour the fragrant fields.

BIG JOHN'S BAR-B-Q
TX 29 and RR 1431. (512) 793-2261

Cash. Order/take out.

Located two miles west of the lakeside community of Buchanan Dam, Big John's is a popular place for picnickers and fishermen looking for a good meal to carry to Lake Buchanan. You'll always find lots of locals here in the screened dining room with its gravel floor and simple picnic tables. The pit is smokin' Thursday through Sundays only, so plan your visits here carefully.

We didn't see John, so we can't attest to his size. But we can say that you'll get a big plate at Big John's. Our favorite is the brisket, sliced thin and tender enough for a baby to chew.

BURNET

Burnet was once the edge of Indian territory. Today the only smoke signals are the ones from the barbecue pit across the road from Fort Croghan. To reach Burnet, travel TX 29 west from I-35 into the hill country.

HILL COUNTRY SMOKEHOUSE
406 E. Polk. (512) 756-2712

Cash/credit.

Although not a restaurant, this is, nevertheless, a popular carryout stop in the hill country for top sausage, ham, bacon, and even jerky. Sausage (several varieties) is their specialty: a mild pork and beef mixture, a spicier pork and beef jalapeño, a pork summer sausage, or a spicy hot link version.

The Hill Country Smokehouse also does custom smoking of beef, pork, mutton, venison, and cabrito.

BURNET COUNTY BARBECUE
AND CENTRAL TEXAS CATERING
TX 29 W. (512) 756-6468

Cash. Order/pick up. Catering.

If you're at the Burnet Chamber of Commerce or historic Fort Croghan, look across the road. See the smoke coming from that ramshackle building? The one with the faded sign and the large painted cactus out front? That's the place. Look both ways crossing the street, then make your way to Burnet County Barbecue. Once you get closer, you'll notice that this is no decrepit shack but a restaurant duded up to look like a joint on its last legs. And the smoke is a signal that there's some mighty serious barbecue brewin' here.

Step up to the counter and order yourself a plate of chicken, pork ribs, sliced brisket, or Elgin sausage (fresh from the Southside Market). All plates are served with beans and potato salad or coleslaw. Take your plate to the dining room decorated with a collection of gimme caps or to the picnic tables outside.

If you're getting your food to go, you can order by the pound: chicken, sausage, pork ribs, ham, brisket, or even goat by special order. Burnet County Barbecue also sells beef jerky and jalapeño cheese by the pound, and tamales by the dozen.

DEL VALLE

A southeast suburb of Austin, Del Valle was until recently the home of Bergstrom Air Force Base. The flyboys are gone, but Del Valle still soars with the heavenly scent of Vic's barbecue.

VIC'S B-B-Q
2751 Bastrop Hwy. (512) 389-1113

Cash. Order/take out. Catering.

About five years ago, Vic Murrieta traded in the red tape of a state job for the red hot coals of his own barbecue joint. Vic was always entering barbecue cook-offs, and folks kept telling him to open his own restaurant. Well, fortunately for Austin barbecue lovers, Vic took their advice. Today his restaurant, located a few minutes southeast of town in Del Valle, serves up award-winning ribs (beef, pork, and baby back), plus a Vic specialty: roasted corn. Every year, Vic takes the huge green corn roaster out to the Rib Ticklin' Affair, the rib festival at Austin's Town Lake, and sells out as fast as he can make the hot ears.

Besides ribs and roasted corn, look for catfish, barbecued chicken, Elgin sausage, brisket, and burgers on the menu at Vic's. It's a joint the proprietor calls "a down to earth place," located 10 minutes from downtown Austin. You can have lunch and dinner here Monday through Saturday, and breakfast as well Wednesday through Saturday.

DRIFTWOOD

Ask any Texan where Driftwood is and you'll get a blank look. Ask where The Salt Lick is, though, and you'll see eyes light up. This restaurant, located a half hour southwest of Austin, is beloved by barbecue buffs and for good reason. The food is tasty, and the atmosphere is genuine.

The Salt Lick is located in the country southwest of Austin. Take US 290 west through Oak Hill and turn left at RR 1826. Continue for 13 miles. The Salt Lick is located directly across from Camp Ben McCulloch, formerly the annual reunion ground for Confederate veterans in the area.

THE SALT LICK
FM 1826 (southwest of Austin). (512) 444-8687

Cash. Table service.

Two things make The Salt Lick unique; the first is its cooking pit. This restaurant boasts one of the few open pits left in the state, plopped right down in the middle of the restaurant for all to see. There's no questioning whether the meat is really smoked here or perhaps sneaked into an oven; you can see (and smell) it for yourself.

The sauce is the second aspect of The Salt Lick that everyone discusses—ya' either love it or hate it. Real barbecue hardliners sometimes object to the sauce because it has a slight Oriental taste. If so, it comes by it honestly: The owner is of Hawaiian descent. His mother, Hisako Roberts, founded the restaurant in the late sixties and developed the secret sauce. We think it's great, and from the size of The Salt Lick's crowds, so do a lot of others.

The sauce is used in both the potato salad (really) and on the meats. Because the meat is cooked on an open pit, the flavor is less smoky than meat cooked in a closed smoker, subtler but still hinting at its trial by fire. You can select from brisket, chicken, and beef and pork ribs, all cooked over oak. We dined here with a group and enjoyed family-style service, with side orders of coleslaw, beans, and potato salad.

The Salt Lick is in a dry precinct, but diners are permitted to bring ice chests stocked with beer and wine. The restaurant is open only Thursday through Sunday, afternoons and evenings.

ELGIN

Around Texas, the name Elgin is synonymous with sausage. The product of this town is sold in barbecue joints through the state. Spicy Elgin sausage is the standard against which other Texas sausages are judged. Elgin is located east of Austin on US 290.

BIGGER'S BARBECUE
US 290. (512) 285-3402

Cash. Order/pick up.

Bigger's is better. This restaurant elevates sausage making to a fine art, churning out some of Elgin's best. Elgin hot links are legendary in Texas, and with companies like the Southside Market and Meyers Sausage in town, it's not easy for a newcomer to gain ground.

But Bigger's has done exactly that, developing a devoted clientele who travel from far and wide to stock up on this all-beef sausage. And with good reason. These hot links are coarsely ground, filled with peppery goodness. We find the casing easier to chew than some others.

Besides the sausage, we also like the ribs and brisket with side dishes of beans and potato salad. You can have your meal in the dining room filled with local residents who know good sausage when they taste it.

CROSSTOWN BBQ
211 Central Ave. (512) 285-9308

Cash. Order/pick up.

Crosstown is located just down the street from the old Southside Market in a part of town filled with century-old buildings, the kind that give a barbecue joint atmosphere like no mere modern structure can. And, in good old-fashioned barbecue style, the no-frills decor includes touches like old metal folding chairs.

But atmosphere never satisfied anyone's appetite—barbecue does. Sample Crosstown's own sausage, an all-beef spicy version that holds up the Elgin name. Or tender brisket, crusty pork ribs, moist chicken, or even a little different fare: mutton ribs. We tried the sausage as well as the pork ribs, the specialty of the house, and found them tender and flavorful, spiked with a spicy rub that any pork lover would enjoy.

SOUTHSIDE MARKET AND B-B-Q, INC.
1212 US 290 W. (512) 281-4650
Cash. Order/pick up.

The Southside Market is probably one of the top five most recognized names in Texas barbecue lore. In business since 1882, the market is known for its Elgin hot sausage, sometimes known as Elgin Hot Guts. However you refer to it, you have to call this sausage good. The mainstay in many barbecue restaurants around the state, the Southside's product is what many people have in mind when they order sausage. Spicy but not hot, the coarse concoction is all beef, greasy, and always good.

Besides sausage, Southside sells brisket, beef and pork ribs, beef steak, pork, and even mutton. Plates are served with potato salad and beans.

For generations, this establishment was located downtown by the railroad tracks. Like places such as Louis Mueller's in Taylor and Kreuz Market in Lockhart, the smoky dining room spoke volumes about barbecue. Today the old building sits vacant, a sad victim of progress. As Southside Market grew, its clientele could no longer fit in its old home. Located now on the highway in an enormous red tin building with a concrete floor, this is one of the largest barbecue joints in the state. The sausage is still good, but the atmosphere just ain't the same.

GEORGETOWN

This quiet bedroom community is located a half hour north of Austin via Interstate 35.

DONN'S TEXAS STYLE BBQ
Leander Rd. and Austin Ave. (512) 863-2299
Cash. Order/pick up.

There's nothing fancy about this little barbecue joint, tucked in a strip center at the southern edge of Georgetown. Especially clean for a smokehouse, the place offers a fine little dining room decorated with framed burlap potato sacks. Nice but not really notable. But then take a bite of the beef ribs. Or the brisket. Or the sausage. You'll be transported to beef and pork lovers' paradise. This Georgetown hideaway has some of the best barbecue in Central Texas, with good side dishes as well.

Brisket is the all-time popular favorite here, sold as plates as well as family packs. But we think that the beef ribs are Donn's best creation. As tender as baby back ribs, we found ourselves thinking fondly about these ribs days after eating here. Ask for the sauce on the side (you don't want to drown this smoky wonder), grab hold with both hands, then dig into ribs that can't be beat.

If sausage is your preference, order a spicy Elgin sausage plate, with beans and potato salad on the side, or order it wrapped with a slice of white bread. Donn's also serves chicken halves, ham, and pork loin. They're all served up with an excellent crunchy potato salad tinged with mustard and a portion of spicy pinto beans.

GRUENE

The once-separate community of Gruene is now incorporated into New Braunfels. For a review of Gruene's barbecue restaurant (the Guadalupe Smoked Meat Company), see the New Braunfels section.

JOHNSON CITY

The eyes of the world were once focused on this hill country town thanks to its most famous resident: Lyndon Baines Johnson. The leader's boyhood home still stands in Johnson City, but he and his first lady actually resided on a ranch in nearby Stonewall. To reach Johnson City, travel north from San Antonio on US 281 or west of I-35 on US 290.

THE HILL COUNTRY CUPBOARD
101 US 281 S. (210) 868-4625
Cash. Table service / take out. Catering.

Traveling north on US 281 from Blanco to Johnson City, you'll start seeing the billboards for The Hill Country Cupboard proclaiming it the best barbecue in the world. With a boast like that, we had to see for ourselves.

It may be a little much to say this is the best in the world (or even in Central Texas), but the product of this country cafe is mighty tasty. We had the brisket plate with that Southern favorite, fried okra, alongside ranch beans and some excellent corn bread muffins that added a sweet touch to the meal. The brisket was served lean and tender. There's also a sausage (a combination of beef and pork) plate served with a choice of eight side dishes, including potato salad, slaw, and country cafe specialties like mashed potatoes and lettuce salad.

UNCLE KUNKEL'S BAR B Q
208 US 281 S. (210) 868-7074
Cash. Order/pick up. Catering.

This is a mom-and-pop operation at its best. Ray and Rosie Kunkel have been barbecuing for years, providing all the catering for the LBJ Ranch and for Mrs. Johnson. Word has it that Mrs. Johnson names the Kunkels' ribs her favorite, stopping by to pick up an order along with slaw and potato salad.

It's easy to see why the former first lady is so smitten with this barbecue. Try the prize-winning pork ribs, brisket, or sausage, or one of the other meats available by special order. They're all winners in our book. If you order by the plate, the meal comes with homemade potato salad, coleslaw, and pinto beans. Save room, because there's usually fresh pie available as well.

The Kunkels offer a small country-style dining room, but get here early. Their barbecue is available only on weekends, and when it's sold out, the door is closed.

LA GRANGE

To much of the country, La Grange is known as the home of "The Best Little Whorehouse in Texas." Well, the brothel is long gone, but the temptations of the flesh remain—at least in the form of beef and pork. La Grange boasts several old-fashioned pits in an atmosphere that's 100% small-town Texas.

PRAUSE'S MARKET
US 77 (on the square). (409) 968-3259
Cash. Order/pick up.

Prause's is the best known barbecue joint in La Grange, a typical meat market eatery that exemplifies the true spirit of Texas barbecue. When folks are in the La Grange area, they head to Prause's as a regular stop, just like getting gas in the pickup truck or stamps at the post office.

Step inside Prause's and walk up to the long meat counter to place your order for fresh meat cuts, or head back beyond the green lattice to order brisket and sausage. The brisket is tender and imbued with smoky flavor, and the sausage is slightly spicy and peppery. Order up a plate and take it to the plain tables, sprinkle it with pepper sauce, and dig in. This is Texas barbecue at its best.

Don't plan to just stroll into Prause's at any time. When these folks run out of barbecue, they close the doors. We went by at one o'clock one Saturday afternoon and found the place locked. And on Sundays, you'll find the sign reads "Gone to Fish."

PRIME BAR-B-Q AND CATERING
Hwy. 159 and 71 Bypass Feeder Rd. (409) 968-8033
Cash. Order / pick up.

Prime Bar-B-Q is a no-nonsense kind of place. The menu is on a board over the window. Your dining accommodations are a picnic table in a lattice-shaded pavilion. You eat off of Styrofoam under the watchful gaze of a framed John Wayne photo. That plastic plate holds a mound of barbecue that any Texas pit would be proud to serve The Duke. Whether you order brisket, pork ribs, sausage, or chicken, you're in for a smoky delight. As good as all the meats are, though, what's really prime here are the ribs. One bite of this fall-off-the-bone tender porcine delicacy, and it's easy to see why.

"We can't keep enough ribs here," says Prime Bar-B-Q co-owner Craig Popp. "We cook with our heat directly under our meat, the old-fashioned way." The meat is cooked over a combination of mesquite, oak, and pecan woods, which Popp says accounts for its unique flavor. Besides ribs, the place also sells a lot of boneless pork loin during the winter months. The sauce is fairly mild, but if you're looking to spice up your meal, give it a splash of the watery mixture on the table. These bottles are filled with tiny round red peppers known locally as bird's eye peppers. Just behind the smokehouse, Popp picks peppers in the pasture (try saying that with a mouthful of brisket), tosses it in a bottle with a few herbs, and tops it all off with vinegar. The result is a pepper sauce that's hot enough to have you smokin'.

Prime Bar-B-Q also offers a smorgasbord of side dishes: macaroni salad, potato salad, baked potato salad, coleslaw, green or pinto beans, or banana pudding.

Popp started in the barbecue business at local cook-offs, but about two years ago decided to enter the pit professionally. "I decided that instead of spending a couple of hundred dollars entering the cook-offs, I'd make a couple of hundred dollars selling it!" he explains. With barbecue this tasty, he should make a whole lot more than that.

LAMPASAS

Lampasas is located northwest of Austin and west of Temple at the intersection of US 183 and US 281.

FULLER'S BAR-B-Q
204 S. Walnut. (512) 556-8392

Cash. Order/pick up. Catering.

How full are the Fullers? We can't speak for owners John and Jeanne, but after a recent visit we were stuffed with some excellent 'que that was so good we wished we had room for more. Tucked back off US 183, Fuller's is located in a building that could masquerade as an antique shop. Covered with weathered barn siding, the two-story restaurant looks like a good place to purchase a battered washstand or a handmade quilt.

But instead go in and buy a brisket or a ham—or at least a plateful served up with homemade potato salad, slaw, or cowboy beans. We like the tender brisket, but we found the peppered ham truly exceptional, a step above the often all-too-mild versions sold by many restaurants. You can also order plates of mesquite-smoked sausage, turkey breast, and pork ribs. Fuller's even offers smoked duck by the pound. We didn't have a chance to try those offerings, but now we have a good excuse to return and fill up on Fuller's again.

LLANO

In the 1880s Llano was a boom town, filled with rock hounds in search of minerals: garnet, amethyst, and even gold. Today the gold is found in this hill country town's barbecue joints. Like Elgin, Lockhart, and Taylor, Llano is one of the hot spots on the Texas barbecue scene. What makes Llano unique is its cooking style. Pitmasters in this town don't smoke their meats. (In fact, smoking may even be a dirty word in these parts.) Instead, Llano's product is the result of indirect barbecuing. Wood, primarily mesquite, is placed in the firebox and allowed to burn down to coals, then it's transferred to the main section of the pit beneath the meat. Here it flavors and cooks the meat to perfection, imparting a delicate smoky taste that is subtler than what you might achieve through ordinary smoking.

But judge for yourself. There are four excellent pits in town, three located within blocks of each other on Texas 29. Just follow the smoke.

BROTHER'S BAR-B-QUE
406 W. Young (TX 29 W.). (915) 247-3003

Cash/credit. Order/pick up. Catering.

It's not too common to see a barbecue restaurant and a service station sharing the same building. But then, there's nothing too common about Brother's. Its tasty offerings are definitely uncommonly good, even in a small town where good barbecue is more prevalent than good ranch land, good deer hunting, and good weather.

Brother's is the operation of Jack Graham, whose brother Ben runs the service station. When you're ready for a fill-up on good barbecue, stop by and give this joint a try. But leave yourself some extra time. The menu, posted on a signboard and spilling out onto half a dozen sheets of paper tacked to the wall, is extensive. Brisket trimmed and untrimmed. Pork steak. Chopped beef. Pork ribs. Chicken half. Chicken whole. Plates served with salad, beans, and tea. The list goes on.

That's just the barbecue offerings. It doesn't include the fried chicken, the burgers, the specials, the side orders.

There's an indoor dining room and also outdoor tables around the smokers if you don't mind smelling like you were being smoked for lunch. Tables are topped with squirt bottles of white vinegar for those who like their barbecue tart.

COOPER'S OLD TIME PIT BARBECUE AND CATERING
604 W. Young (TX 29 W.). (915) 247-5713

Cash. Order/pick up. Catering.

Cooper's is the legacy of the late Tommy Cooper, whose father operated another Cooper's in Mason. (The Cooper family also has the Cooper's Old-Time Pit Barbecue in Round Rock.) During Tommy Cooper's reign over what many consider to be Llano's best barbecue joint, local pitmaster Kenneth Laird worked alongside the master. Today Laird has his own Llano restaurant: Laird's Bar-B-Q Pit.

You won't find a more genuine-looking barbecue joint in Texas than Cooper's. From its huge rectangular pits located by the front door to the dining room lined with loaves of white bread and jars of jalapeño peppers, this is the real thing. The Cooper's experience, however, begins before you ever step inside. As you travel down Texas 29 toward Mason, you'll smell the place before you see it. The aroma from the huge pits tempts travelers better than any mere billboard ever could.

Before entering the restaurant you'll walk past those pits, but don't be in any hurry. This is where you place your order. The pitmaster opens the huge pits to reveal a king's treasure: brisket, pork ribs, beef ribs, chicken, goat, sausage, sirloin steak, and pork chops. Select what you want and how much you want. The pit man will carve it off and drop it on some butcher paper for you to take inside for weighing. There you can pick up some potato salad or chips, then head to the cinderblock dining room. Here simple rows of picnic tables are topped with white bread and condiments. This room is usually filled with Llano locals, deer hunters, and travelers alike.

In the back of the dining room, cauldrons hold pinto beans and sauce. Help yourself. The sauce is tart with vinegar, a thin concoction that makes a good dip for the white bread that's yours for the taking.

When you're done, just drop your silverware in the utility sink and head reluctantly on your way.

INMAN'S KITCHEN AND CATERING SERVICE
809 W. Young (TX 29 W.). (915) 247-5257
Cash. Order/pick up. Catering.

Llano is the heart of the Texas deer country, so you might expect venison sausage to be the star attraction in this eatery. Think again. Here the almighty deer is overshadowed by the turkey. Turkey sausage is king at Inman's, and after a few bites it's easy to see why. The sausage is mild and less greasy than its beef and pork cousins, but with all the flavor and texture.

Not in the mood for turkey? Then try the beef brisket (it's tender enough to cut with a fork), chicken, or pork ribs. The plates come with beans and potato salad or coleslaw. There's also a good selection of sandwiches made with beef, turkey sausage, or ham. Save room for homemade pies.

Inman's is definitely the most citified barbecue spot in Llano. The gussied-up dining room is air conditioned and carpeted, even furnished with matching chairs. It may be a little too pretty for some of the die-hard barbecue buffs, but it's a nice place to go when you don't want to smell like smoke.

Today the pit is no longer owned by an Inman, but the restaurant still serves up a product much like that which Lester Inman once sold. The nephew of the original owner has his own barbecue joint, Inman's Ranch House Barbecue (see the Marble Falls section). He sells turkey sausage as well.

LAIRD'S BAR-B-Q PIT RESTAURANT AND CATERING SERVICE
1404 Ford St. (915) 247-5234

Cash. Order/pick up. Catering.

Don't look for Laird's on the side of the highway or in some strip center. This not-to-be-missed joint is tucked in a neighborhood off TX 16, just south of the bridge crossing the Llano River. But we don't need to worry about giving you directions. Follow the smoke and the smell of some of Llano's best barbecue. If it's lunchtime, follow the pickup trucks of Llano's workmen. They're probably headed to Laird's.

Most days you'll find Kenneth Laird behind the counter of this popular joint, taking orders and carving meat. The former employee of Cooper's now serves up some of Llano's finest to a dining room full of regulars who sit in the small, air-conditioned dining room and talk about the comings and goings in town.

We enjoyed excellent sliced beef accompanied by beans and potato salad, all served up by Laird himself. The menu also offers sausage, pork, chicken, and steaks.

LOCKHART

Located 23 miles south of Austin on US 183, Lockhart's nickname is "The Barbecue Capital of Texas." Black's and the Kreuz Market are longtime shrines for many barbecue buffs; Chisholm Trail is a new entry that has already picked up many devoted fans. You won't find an article on Texas barbecue without mention of this little town. Some folks swear Lockhart smokes up the best barbecue in the state. You'll have a lot of fun judging for yourself.

BLACK'S BARBECUE
215 N. Main St. (512) 398-2712

Cash. Cafeteria style.

Black's claims to be the oldest barbecue house in Texas continually owned by the same family. Since 1932 the Black family has been firing up these brick pits every day for lunch and dinner. Today, Norma and Edgar Black tend the post oak fires to provide Lockhart meat eaters with the stuff this town is famous for.

This is a sit-down restaurant, a little prettier than most smoky joints. Decorated with Texas paraphernalia and photos of high school football teams, Black's is a comfortable place to enjoy some of Lockhart's finest. You can select from brisket, pork ribs, chicken, and ham, or try Black's own homemade beef and pork sausage with a ladleful of caramel-colored sauce on the side.

CHISHOLM TRAIL
US 183 (south side of town). (512) 398-6027

Cash/credit. Cafeteria style. Catering.

It's not easy to open a barbecue restaurant in Lockhart—how do you compete with the likes of Kreuz Market and Black's? With great prices and great food, that's how. For under $4, you can enjoy a big meal at this joint, open daily for lunch and dinner. The folks are friendly, the barbecue is tasty, and the side dishes are reason enough to make this a regular stop.

Those side dishes are a unique aspect at Chisholm Trail. The restaurant boasts a hot and cold food bar stocked with dozens of items: potato salad, coleslaw, broccoli salad, macaroni and cheese, corn, green beans, black-eyed peas, Jello salad, pinto beans—the list goes on and on.

But the best reason to stop at Chisholm Trail is the barbecue, tender smoke-filled meat that holds up the Lockhart tradition. Brisket, sausage, ham, chicken, pork and beef ribs, and even fajitas are house specialties here.

KREUZ MARKET
208 S. Commerce St. (512) 398-2361

Cash. Order/pick up.

If you want to sound like a real Texan, you have to know how to pronounce Kreuz. No, don't say "Cruise." It's "Krites," rhyming with "lights." This smoky barbecue joint is known by Texans around the state who make regular pilgrimages to feast on this meat. And meat is about all that's on the menu. Don't look for side orders here. No beans. No potato salad. No coleslaw. Not even any banana pudding. Just meat, meat, and more meat, some of the best Central Texas has to offer.

Kreuz's has been in the barbecue business since 1948, and the thousands of pounds this pit has turned out have helped give the town of Lockhart its title as "The Barbecue Capital of Texas." The market was started by the Kreuz family in 1900 and later operated by the Schmidts. Today Don Schmidt, son of "Smitty" Schmidt who bought the joint in 1948, tends the pits. Like his father before him, Don sells barbecue shoulder clod, a cut that's leaner than brisket and also cooks faster. Brisket, pork loin, and prime rib are also for sale here.

No matter what kind of meat you order, it will be cooked in the huge pits system devised by "Smitty" Schmidt. Two brick pits burn oak logs, and a 35-foot chimney draws smoke over the meat, which does not sit directly over the fire. Your meal is served on a piece of rosy-brown butcher paper. Your silverware is a plastic knife. And your side dishes consist of a half package of saltines and some jalapeños, cheese, pickles, onions, or, the true mark of a barbecue joint, white bread.

To escape the heat of those pits, Kreuz's now features two air-conditioned dining rooms. Some of the locals still like to sit in the old section, filled with smoke and heat. Give it a try and feel like a real Texan. Don't forget, though, to say "Krites" when you tell everyone where you ate that good barbecue.

LULING

Located on US 90 just off I-10 east of San Antonio, Luling is the land of oil wells. Although this area's heyday as a boomtown is gone, pumpjacks are still seen throughout town, and the barbecue restaurants are still pumping out their own version of black gold.

LULING CITY MARKET
633 Davis St. (210) 875-9019

Cash. Order/pick up.

This is small-town barbecue the way it ought to be: served up in a no-frills smoky meat market, with ambience replaced by plenty of local atmosphere. The Luling City Market has been in business longer than anyone can remember, turning out smoked brisket, sausage, ribs, and mutton.

If you've ventured down to Houston, you'll know the big city sports its own version of the Luling City Market, even using the same recipes as this small-town joint. But for the real thing you have to come to the source, where smoke-tinted walls and no-nonsense barbecue bring in both the oil field workers and the oil field owners.

MARBLE FALLS

The hill country town of Marble Falls is best known for the pink granite it yielded to construct the state capitol. This lakeside community located at the intersection of US 281 and RR 1431 has another claim to fame: It's the long-time home of a barbecue joint owned by a member of the Inman barbecue dynasty.

INMAN'S RANCH HOUSE BARBECUE AND TURKEY SAUSAGE
US 281 and Sixth St. (210) 693-2711
Cash. Order/pick up.

Billy Inman's late uncle founded the original Inman's up in Llano, which specialized in turkey sausage. Billy followed in his uncle's footsteps and opened this Inman's three decades ago. The menu is simple here. Billy and Francis Inman sell brisket and turkey sausage with sides of coleslaw and beans. That's it. Take it or leave it.

The Ranch House Barbecue is located in an old house, with a few simple tables tucked in former bedrooms and the living room. You place your order in the back room of the house, where you can get a peek at the huge red pit where the Inmans work their magic.

We tried everything on the menu (not such a difficult task), and we can say that everything is a winner. The brisket is full of smoky taste, a testimony to long hours in that big red pit. The turkey sausage is less greasy than its beef and pork cousins, and full of spicy goodness.

NEW BRAUNFELS

Some folks think that New Braunfels, located 35 miles northeast of San Antonio on I-35, is the sausage capital of Texas. The earliest residents of this town were German immigrants who used every part of a swine when butchered, even some of the less appetizing ones. As one New Braunfels museum puts it, "They used everything but the squeal." To make use of those less desirable cuts of meat, markets began to make sausage. Today, the town celebrates that heritage of hot links with Wurstfest. This late October and early November blowout is one of the largest German festivals in the country, brimming with brew, bratwurst, and usually even some barbecue. And if you don't make it down to New Braunfels for Wurstfest, you can always find plenty of good barbecue and sausage any day of the year at one of the several excellent joints in town.

GRANZIN BAR-B-Q
954 W. San Antonio St. (210) 629-6615
Cash. Take out.

Slow down on San Antonio Street or you might miss Granzin's. And that would be a shame. It might not look like much, housed in a little one-room building, but pass it by and you'll pass up some good eatin'. Granzin's has been in business nearly a decade, and it's a favorite with New Braunfels locals who line up at lunch and dinner six days a week (it's closed on Sundays) to pick up some tender meat and flavorful side dishes. The motto of Granzin's, found on the restaurant sign and even on mugs for sale, is "It's the sauce and the wood." That's as good an explanation as any of what makes this barbecue special.

Owner Miles Granzin keeps the pits stocked with mesquite, which accounts for the flavor. He cooks his brisket over eight hours, and says that it's the most popular dish in the house. "We serve a little bit of everything here," says Granzin. The menu, painted on a board beside the walk-up window, is lengthy. You can pick from sliced beef, chopped beef, sausage, ham, chicken breast, and turkey breast sandwiches. Hungrier? Pick a plate with beef, ribs (beef, pork, or pork country-style), ham, sausage, or chicken, plus beans and potato salad. Or go for the tacos, a combination that brings together the best of barbecue and Tex-Mex into an easy-to-hold lunch. Taco combinations include chopped or sliced beef, sausage and cheese, turkey breast, or chicken breast.

No matter what you select, don't miss the potato salad. "We're well known for our potato salad," brags Granzin. "It doesn't taste like anybody else's potato salad. We sell tons of it." Try a bite and you'll see this is no idle boast. Crunchy and packed with flavor, this is a potato salad to write home about.

GUADALUPE SMOKED MEAT COMPANY
1299 Gruene Rd. (210) 629-6121

Cash / credit. Table service. Catering.

In 1984 Janie Macredie opened the Guadalupe Smoked Meat Company in the historic village of Gruene (pronounced "Green"). At one time, Gruene had been a roaring town on the banks of the Guadalupe River. Started in the 1870s, the community was prosperous until the boll weevil made the cotton industry shrivel up like the cotton bolls in the fields.

But Janie Macredie felt like Gruene was a community whose time had come again. So she started the Guadalupe Smoked Meat Company, becoming one of the first independent businesses to pump life back into this former ghost town on the outskirts of New Braunfels. Janie was right. Today Gruene is a popular weekend haven, filled with shoppers and outdoor buffs who come to enjoy antique shops, bed-and-breakfast inns, and river rafting on the Guadalupe River. And to enjoy a great barbecue joint.

Guadalupe Smoked Meat Company sets the standards by which other Texas barbecue is judged. It just doesn't get better than this. Smoked over green hickory, the meat is flavorful and tender, the sauce is spicy but not overpowering, and the restaurant is located in one of Central Texas's most beautiful outdoor spots. What more do you want?

We know what we want. We want to go back. Again and again. We'd start with the smoked sausage, a garlicky appetizer served sliced with a side of sauce and spicy mustard. From there, we'd move on to what Guadalupe Smoked Meats calls the "Basic 'Q' Plates." Paris would choose the pork spareribs, St. Louis–style cuts that are meaty and tender just like any pork lover would want; John would select the brisket, a choice that the restaurant swears is tender enough to cut with a fork. Don't even bother to pick up your knife—like the owner says, you don't need it.

Plates are served with a choice of two side dishes. The pinto beans, seasoned with jalapeños and cumin, have to be the first choice. It's a tough battle for second, fought between Elly's Cole Slaw, a crunchy slaw that's not sweet but oh, so good, and the Old-Fashioned Potato Salad, made with mayonnaise. If you're in the mood for something different, have the half avocado with picante sauce, some pico de gallo, a salad, Texas fries, or, to give your taste buds a jump start, two jalapeños.

Guadalupe offers plenty of other temptations on the menu, including burgers, smoked turkey sandwiches, a B.A.L.T. (bacon, avocado, lettuce, and tomato), and barbecue tacos made with brisket or chicken. There's even wine on the menu, but don't get nervous. Most of it is Texas wine, so that kind of makes up for any snootiness you might be worried about. There are also plenty of longnecks to balance things out.

If you want to finish off with something sweet, you've got another difficult decision ahead: blackberry cobbler topped with Texas's own Blue Bell ice cream, an old-fashioned sarsaparilla float, or, our favorite, the Guadalupe Mud Cake, a brownie-type cake topped with marshmallow creme and fudge.

You can enjoy all this heavenly fare in the original Gruene location, housed in the former Rodriguez Family General Store, a historic building moved to Gruene from the community of Martindale. The Gruene restaurant has a beautiful deck under the trees, some of the best outdoor dining in the state.

If you just don't want to leave the house, pick up the phone and have some of the Guadalupe's barbecue shipped to you (see Appendix B: Barbecue Gifts and Products for more details).

KENO'S BARBECUE AND RESTAURANT
1050 S. Seguin at US 81.(210) 625-1611

Cash. Cafeteria style / take out. Catering.

You can't miss Keno's. Look for the antique car, rusted down to a hunk of metal, sitting out front. Since Keno's is located in New Braunfels, the town that calls itself the "Antique Capital of Texas," it's pretty fitting that the restaurant helps out with a few antiques of its own. In business almost two and a half decades, the eatery itself is moving up to antique status thanks to a loyal local following through the years.

Inside the etched-glass front doors, you'll find more antiques, all displayed on walls paneled with weathered barn siding. Lit by wagon-wheel chandeliers, you might feel like you're walking into an Old West saloon when you saunter into this restaurant. Mosey on up to the bar, have a look over the smoked meats, and give your order. It's that simple. You can't go wrong, because Keno's offers good food and lots of it.

Stop by at midday for the weekday lunch special, a choice of brisket, sausage, or chicken plus two side dishes: coleslaw, beans, or potato salad. The potato salad is crunchy and seasoned with plenty of pepper and chopped onions. We especially enjoyed the beans, spicier than most and spiked with a little smoky flavor that complemented the barbecue. Wash it all down with iced tea served in quart-sized glasses.

What makes this barbecue special is the dry seasoning and hours over mesquite. The brisket is tender and sliced thin, slathered in a sauce that's slightly sweet. The restaurant also sells a lot of chicken and ribs, plus Keno's own sausage, a combination pork and beef that's mild and not too greasy.

Keno's also has tacos and sandwiches for the lunch crowd, plus home-made pies for those who've saved room. Select apple, cherry, or that Texas favorite, pecan, to finish off your meal.

NEW BRAUNFELS SMOKEHOUSE
TX 46 and US 81. (210) 609-0100

Cash / credit. Table service / take out. Catering.

Mill Store Plaza #420, 651 Hwy. 81 E. (210) 620-7905

Cash / credit. Order / pick up.

If you get the chance to go to Wurstfest, you'll undoubtedly sample the product of the New Braunfels Smokehouse. For this fall event, the smokehouse produces between 40,000 and 60,000 pounds of sausage. That's a lot of links, but it's not an unmanageable order for a business that smokes up to 500 turkeys and 400 hams daily.

All the meats here are smoked over hickory, just as they have been since the Dunbar family started the business in 1943. At that time, R. K. Dunbar bought an old ice plant where customers could store their meats and have them custom smoked. That meat became so popular that in 1951 the family opened up a "Tastin' Kitchen" for customers to sample the product. So much tastin' took place that the family soon constructed a 300-seat restaurant in New Braunfels, followed by two mall locations (see the San Antonio section) and a mail order business that ships over 600,000 catalogs to sausage lovers all over the country (see Appendix B).

The restaurants have a little of everything, including smoked ham and brisket sandwiches with coleslaw or potato salad. We especially liked the combination plate of tender beef brisket and sausage (either kielbasa or bratwurst) served with pinto beans, German potato salad, and homemade bread. Save room for the bread pudding here, a comforting mixture of bread, raisins, brown sugar, and lots of butter.

ROUND ROCK

Just north of Austin on I-35, Round Rock is a bedroom community for Austin employees. Before those workers head home, many stop by one of Round Rock's pits to pick up a tasty dinner or family pack.

BOB'S BAR-B-Q ETC.
1601 S. I-35. (512) 255-4840
Cash/credit. Table service/take out. Catering.

Bob's is a place that knows barbecue and Texans. You can tell by the sign hanging over the counter: "Bar-b-que, sex and death are subjects that provoke intense speculation in most Texans. Of the three, probably bar-b-que is taken most seriously." One thing's for sure—Bob's takes its barbecue seriously, and there's something here to please any barbecue lover. All meats are served with a spicy barbecue sauce that has won the owner (yes, his name is Bob) awards in several barbecue cook-offs.

Tender beef brisket is a big winner here, as well as baby back pork ribs. Both are popular favorites. There's also pork tenderloin, ham, chicken, beef ribs, and Elgin sausage. Reward yourself with a plate of any of these smoky delights; each is served with Texas toast and two homemade side dishes. The choice includes beans, corn on the cob, potato salad, fried okra, coleslaw, french fries, garden salad, or even french-fried corn. Haven't heard of french-fried corn? It's a half ear of corn, batter dipped and deep fried, an excellent dish that's pretty unique to Bob's.

Bob's has plenty of sandwiches for the lunch crowd, including one called a Jal-A-Que. It's a spicy concoction made of sliced brisket chopped with jalapeños and combined with barbecue sauce.

Most days, you'll find Bob and wife Joy in the restaurant they've owned for nearly 10 years. It's a friendly place, the kind of small-town spot where locals run into each other as they dine out or pick up dinner.

COOPER'S PIT BAR-B-Q AND CATERING
403 N. Mays. (512) 255-5638
Cash/credit. Order/pick up. Catering.

Cooper's is a place with a lot of rules. Posted on the brick wall are hand-lettered admonitions: absolutely no profanity, must be 16 years old to play on pool tables, no jump shots, no slamming balls on table, no sitting on pool tables. The list goes on. Actually, Cooper's could make do with one rule: Eat here. The owners are related to the owners of the hill country Cooper's up in Llano, another fine pit.

This restaurant is a genuine greasehouse, so authentic, in fact, it almost looks like a movie set. But this is the real thing, all right, from the smoking pits located outside by the front door to the mismatched tables to the walls dotted with trophy fish and deer—one sporting a sombrero. Of course, the only way to really identify a true smokehouse is to try its product. Step up to the counter, have a look at the long list of smoked meats, and make your selection.

We liked the beef and pork ribs and the brisket. The smoked turkey is excellent as well, filled with the smoky essence of the pits outside. (Unfortunately, the smoked turkey is kept refrigerated and microwaved on order.) You can also select ham, chicken, spicy Elgin sausage, pork chops, or even sirloin. All are served with a tomatoey sauce that's watery and is best as a sop for white bread. Jalapeños on the menu liven up those taste buds. There's a full complement of side dishes as well: potato salad, coleslaw, pinto beans, and even macaroni salad.

Plus pool tables. But don't sit on them.

POK-E-JO'S SMOKEHOUSE
1202-C N. I-35. (512) 388-7578
Cash / credit. Order / pick up. Catering.

This country cousin of the popular Austin barbecue joint brings back the flavor of the original Pok-E-Jo's, with horseshoe pits and volleyball courts. Inside, the offerings are like those at the Austin location: smoky beef and pork ribs, brisket, mild or spicy sausage, pork loin, chicken, ham, and sometimes turkey. Smoked 16 to 20 hours over green mesquite, every choice is a winner. (For a full description of Pok-E-Jo's excellent 'que, refer to the Austin section.)

SHADY LANE BARBECUE
N. Mays at Bowman. (512) 388-1222
Cash. Order / pick up / delivery. Catering.

Shady Lane doesn't look like a barbecue joint. It looks more like a sub sandwich shop in a small strip center. But don't let that fool you. From the brisket to the ribs, this is authentic Texas barbecue.

One of the specialties of the house here is brisket. Take one bite and you'll see that this is no idle boast. Don't worry about picking up a knife with the brisket plate; you can cut this with your fork. If you're not in the mood for brisket, order Shady Lane's other specialty: Elgin sausage. You'll also find ham, pork ribs, and smoked chicken to round off the menu.

Plates come with a side order of tangy potato salad, peppery beans, or crunchy coleslaw. And save room for homemade banana pudding or pecan pie.

ROUND TOP

The smallest incorporated city in Texas has only 81 residents, but a good barbecue restaurant nonetheless. Just 90 minutes from Houston, Round Top is located north of La Grange on TX 237. Besides the barbecue restaurant, the town's other dining spot, the Round Top Cafe, is home to an enormous wholesale sauce business that ships pepper sauce to all 50 states. (Plus it's a great place to grab a piece of homemade pie for dessert.)

KLUMP'S
TX 237 (downtown). (409) 249-5696
Cash. Table service.

Like most businesses and homes in tiny Round Top, Klump's is located in a historic building, an 1800s tinsmith shop that was later converted to a country store. Today it's a country cafe owned and operated by the Klump family. Ron and Liz do the cooking, daughter Kristina waits tables, son Russell helps with the barbecue, and Edith "Granny" Klump runs the cash register. The Klumps have been smokin' in Round Top for a decade, first selling barbecue to oil field workers from a downtown grocery store. In 1991 they moved their pit to this restaurant.

Today the family only fires up the pits on Saturdays, when you can order brisket, pork, chicken, pork spare ribs, and sausage with sides of potato salad, coleslaw, and pinto beans. Everything on the menu is homemade. The rest of the week, Klump's does a good burger and steak, plus Mexican food on Wednesdays, catfish on Fridays, and fried chicken on Sundays.

SALADO

This shop-'til-you-drop town is a popular stop for travelers on I-35. Located just south of Temple, this small burg has a good barbecue restaurant and a deli and gift shop on the west side of the interstate.

COWBOY'S BAR-BE-QUE
I-35 exit 285. (817) 947-5700
Cash. Order/pick up. Catering.

When you stop at a restaurant on the interstate highway and see a dining room filled with locals, you know you're in the right place. Cowboy's Bar-Be-Que is that kind of place. Side by side with shoppers and interstate travelers sit Salado residents and workers on their lunch breaks. They're spread out throughout the spacious dining room decorated with photos of country and western performers. We sampled as much as we could hold: the brisket, the sausage, and the pork ribs, saving the chicken for another day. It was all mighty tasty, a testimony to the hours in the smoker that left a vibrant smoke ring just beneath the crusty surface of the brisket. The homemade side dishes were good as well, from fried okra to standbys like pintos, potato salad, and coleslaw.

ROBERTSON'S HAMS AND THE CHOPPIN' BLOCK
I-35 exit 285. (817) 947-5562 or (800) 458-HAMS
Cash / credit. Deli style.

While you're in Salado, stop by this deli and gift shop. It's located just a sausage link's throw from Cowboy's Bar-Be-Que. The shop is filled with kitchen implements, cookbooks, and jars of Robertson's Barbecue Sauce, a dark concoction whose ingredients include molasses.

While you're here, order a smoked ham sandwich or get some to take home. Step up to the meat market counter and order, then head over to the butcher block to fill your sandwich with condiments. If you get home and wish you'd have picked up more of Robertson's smoky product, there's a mail order business as well (see Appendix B for details).

SAN ANTONIO

The Alamo City is the land of tacos and tortillas, gorditas and guacamole. With its strong Hispanic culture, San Antonio is the capital of Tex-Mex cuisine. But every diner needs a break, and when San Antonians need one they evidently head to the local barbecue joint. At last count there were over 90 smokin' pits across town, drawing in gross sales topping $58 million annually. Barbecue is big business here.

BILLY BLUES BARBECUE BAR AND GRILL
330 E. Grayson. (210) 225-7409
Cash / credit. Table service / take out.

You won't be singing the blues after a meal at Billy Blues, but you will hear some. Every night this popular eatery hosts musicians from San Antonio and Austin plus nationally known acts. Blues rules, but two nights a week are reserved for jazz and acoustic acts.

Billy Blues is a San Antonio–based chain of roadhouse barbecue joints with locations in Austin, Dallas, and Houston. Recently the pitmasters opened their first European restaurant, Billy Blues Feinkost in Heidelberg, Germany, with four more German locations planned over the next two years. They're negotiating to spice up Geneva, Moscow, and Dublin as well.

What's the secret? Billy Blues might say the sauce, a concoction used in the restaurants and sold in stores around Texas. It comes from a recipe used by South Texas pioneer Herman Haak, known as the first brewmaster at the Pearl Brewery in San Antonio. The secret ingredient in this sauce isn't beer, though, it's coffee!

Billy's menu is big, starting with "Warm Up Acts" that include "Wings and a Prayer" (barbecued chicken wings), "Lightnin' Bolts" (battered jalapeño peppers), and "Gimme Caps" (fried mushrooms). From there, it's on to more traditional smokehouse fare in the "Hand Jives" sandwich section. Choose a "Pinched Piggy Sandwich" for tender pulled pork shoulder, a "Hard Luck Club" for a barbecue club sandwich made with a combination of chicken, sausage, pulled pork, or brisket, or your usual beef brisket, smoked sausage, or chopped beef sandwich. If your appetites are heartier, look at the "Blues Plate Specials" for pulled pork shoulder, brisket, baby back ribs, chicken, or sausage. We especially liked the baby back ribs, smoked until the meat rolled off the bone, and the brisket, sliced thin and devoid of any traces of fat.

The side dishes here include a chunky, mayonnaise-based potato salad (made with the potato skins on) and a crispy coleslaw that's above average. You'll also find barbecued green beans, curly fries, and the Longneck Cornbake, a dish that will have sweat popping out on your forehead after just a few bites. The problem is, it's so good you keep going back for more. Made with corn, cheese, ham, jalapeños, and a dash of chili pepper, this dish makes a hot complement to the barbecue.

BUN 'N BARREL
1150 Austin Hwy. (210) 828-2829

Cash. Table service / take out / car service. Catering.

If you're nostalgic for the 1950s, visit the Bun 'n Barrel. Founded in 1950, this diner is a genuine product of those happy days, complete with car hops, frothy malts, and a lunch counter. The walls are dotted with photos of classic cars, and a bulletin board by the cash register displays ads offering classic cars and parts. Every Saturday night, oldies enthusiasts fill the Bun 'n Barrel parking lot, swapping stories and making deals on those old jalopies.

But the best reason to visit the Bun 'n Barrel is the barbecue—and the buns. Order the chopped beef sandwich, a finely chopped mixture devoid of fat and seasoned with tangy sauce. It's served up on a homemade braided roll dotted with poppy seeds. If you're in the mood for something else, try the pork ribs, beef sausage, ham, or turkey breast served with potato salad and ranch-style beans.

Watch where you park at the Bun 'n Barrel. Although the sign says "Flash Your Lights for Service," we had a car hop at our door moments after mistakenly pulling into the take-out lot. Also, behind the restaurant there's another Bun 'n Barrel building for take-out orders only.

CLUB HOUSE PIT BAR-B-Q
2218 Broadway. (210) 229-9945

Cash / credit cards. Table service.

This is one clubhouse you don't have to be a member to enter, but after one meal you'll quickly join this restaurant's fan club. From the outside, the Club House looks like a converted hamburger or chicken joint. Inside, the small dining room is neat and unassuming, with checkered tablecloths and brick walls papered with San Antonio Spurs posters and business cards of Club House fans. But take a whiff and you know that you're not in any hamburger hut. That's the smell of slow-cooked barbecue, prepared in a brick pit. All the meats are prepared without tenderizers or MSG—nothing but beef, pork, and chicken and lots of tangy sauce, all served by a friendly wait staff.

The ribs—both pork and beef—are generously cut and fall-off-the-bone tender. The sausage is all beef, tasty but not too spicy. Plates also feature chicken, pork, and beef brisket. Can't decide? Choose the "Super Platter" with a combination of five meats, potato salad, beans, and white bread. It's the best buy in the house and big enough to share. We found it one of the best bargains in Central Texas.

Finally, if anyone has saved room, there's a good supply of desserts. Offerings vary, but you'll usually find peach cobbler, brownies, bread pudding, and even sweet potato pie.

Paul Bunyan appetites should come by on Tuesday or Friday evenings for the all-you-can-eat special. On Friday nights there's live jazz, too, usually with no cover charge. And for those with a hunger for something a little different, like smoked turkey or smoked ham, swing by for the weekday lunch specials. The Club House even has a B-Y-O-M (bring your own meat) feature. You can bring in your own meat, and they'll smoke it for you.

The Club House has some of the best barbecue we've ever eaten, and at some of the best prices. Give it a try—then join the club.

COUNTY LINE BARBECUE
Loop 1604 W., 606 W. Afton Oaks Blvd. (210) 496-0011

Cash/credit. Table service. Catering.

Like its cousins in Austin, this place is one of the nicest barbecue joints in the state, worthy of the term "restaurant." It's a favorite spot for folks going out for a special occasion, even if that occasion is just to celebrate a terrific plate of beef ribs, baby backs, brisket, and sausage. Situated in a Texas farmhouse–style building, this restaurant is set just off busy Loop 410 in a grove of beautiful live oak trees. You'd think you were in the country instead of just seconds from the hustle and bustle of the highway.

Besides the usual County Line specialties, this location serves smoked prime rib and smoked pork tenderloin. (For a full rundown, see the descriptions of the two Austin locations. County Line food is also available by mail order; see the listing in Appendix B.)

DICK'S LAST RESORT
406 Navarro St. (on the River Walk). (210) 224-0026

Cash/credit. Table service.

Dick's is the kind of place that makes some people nervous. It has a reputation as a swinging, fun-loving joint, the sort where the waiters and waitresses like to crack jokes and toss out matchbooks decorated with old photos of topless women. The type of place that suits up its diners with huge plastic bibs that proclaim "I Got Crabs at Dick's" or decorates its ladies' room with photos of scantily clad hunks and vending machines offering fluorescent condoms. But don't be afraid. The waiters and waitresses are actually very attentive, even nice. The bib is practical, especially when you start to wrap your hands around a beef rib that's large enough to have come from a mastodon. And the matchbooks, well, they'll be useful for lighting up conversations even months later.

We really didn't expect to find to find excellent barbecue in this always-packed River Walk eatery that is one of the highest-grossing restaurants in the state of Texas. What we found wasn't just excellent barbecue, it was some of the best we've had. This place serves up the kind of meals that even days later you think about with fond memories, wishing you could go back and order it all over again.

Located in the basement of the former Nix Hospital, the restaurant has both inside and outside seating (the latter is tough to get during good weather, but well worth the wait). If you dine inside, plan to sit at huge communal tables and enjoy some good blues played by some of the area's finest musicians. Don't expect to be handed a menu; the offerings are written on a blackboard. If you have any questions, your waiter (whose name you'll be well acquainted with before you leave) will fill you in on the dishes. There are pork ribs and beef ribs (the largest we've had), barbecue chicken, and barbecue shrimp.

Everything here is served in small tin buckets on a tablecloth of white butcher paper. Don't be shy, just dig in and enjoy. The pork ribs are fall-off-the-bone tender, and the beef ribs are meaty and smoky. The shrimp are jumbo, served three each on a skewer and slathered with sauce. The dishes are served with a bucket of french fries and bread. Save room for the desserts: Mississippi mud pie, cheesecake, and that Texas favorite, pecan pie.

Whether you're in a mood to be cheered up, looking for an excuse to visit the River Walk, or just wanting some unbeatable barbecue, head to Dick's. This restaurant won't be your last resort.

FATSO'S SPORTS GARDEN
1704 Bandera Rd. (210) 432-0121
Cash / credit. Table service / take out.

Plan to spend plenty of time at Fatso's. Crowds and a busy waitstaff at this popular sports bar may very well throw your plans into overtime. But no one said that barbecue was fast food. Give the waitress your order, watch the bartender pour you some suds, then kick back and enjoy sports action from around the globe. Four satellite dishes pick up games and races, broadcasting them on sets sprinkled throughout the restaurant. And if you're not in the mood for TV, there are plenty of pool tables around to create your own sports action.

Barbecue here includes brisket and ribs, good enough to bring even sports haters to this sports bar.

GRADY'S BAR-B-QUE
4109 Fredericksburg. (210) 732-3571
Cash / credit. Cafeteria order / drive through.
7400 Bandera. (210) 684-2899
Cash / credit. Cafeteria order / drive through.

Grady Cowart has been keeping the folks in San Antonio happy with big plates of barbecue since 1948. His restaurants serve up some of the most inexpensive offerings in the region, in large, comfortable dining rooms decorated with cowboy art.

You can choose from beef, sausage, ham, or rib plates. We opted for brisket and ribs and couldn't have been happier. The brisket was tender and thinly sliced, served with a tangy sauce. The ribs were also cooked to tender perfection. All the plates arrive with a corn bread muffin plus a choice of two side dishes: french fries, potato salad, coleslaw, or beans. We didn't have a chance to try the french fries, but the potato salad was flavorful and crisp.

If your hunger is too small for a plate, opt for one of the sandwiches: sliced beef, sausage, ham, or chopped beef. There are also catfish sandwiches, chicken-fried steak sandwiches, and hamburgers. For dessert, there's traditional pecan pie.

BILL MILLER BAR-B-Q
430 Santa Rosa. (210) 302-1510

Cash. Order/pick up.

Many folks in San Antonio and Austin grew up on the barbecue of Bill Miller. With over 35 locations in San Antonio alone, this giant is the largest barbecue chain in the United States. It might be considered the "fast food" of barbecue joints, perhaps with a product milder and more geared to family tastes than some of its competitors, but nevertheless the offerings here are plentiful and inexpensive. Take the whole family and order anything on the menu—brisket, chicken, sausage, or ham, followed by an excellent slice of homemade pie—and you still won't break the family budget.

NEW BRAUNFELS SMOKEHOUSE
Sunset Valley Shopping Center, 6450 N. New Braunfels. (210) 826-6008

Cash/credit. Order/pick up.

San Antonians who are hungry for sausage need not look beyond Sunset Valley Shopping Center. Here, housed in a small mall store, you'll find the best of New Braunfels sausage, prepared by the smokehouse that's been cranking out links since 1943. (For a full description of the New Braunfels Smokehouse, see the New Braunfels section.)

RUDY'S "COUNTRY STORE" AND BAR-B-Q
I-10 at Leon Springs/Boerne Stage Rd. exit. (210) 698-0418

Cash/credit. Order/pick up. Catering.

Rudy's calls itself "the worst bar-b-q in Texas." You sure wouldn't know that from the taste of their product, or from the crowds that flock to this sprawling joint just north of San Antonio in Leon Springs. Mention barbecue in the Alamo City and you'll hear Rudy's name. You can't miss the place—if the smell of smokin' meats doesn't lead you off the interstate, then the fluorescent pink letters atop the joint will. Once you arrive, you'll find an old-fashioned meat market with indoor seating plus an always-packed outdoor area filled with picnic tables holding bottles of vinegar and sauce.

Rudy's has an extensive menu: pork, baby back, St. Louis, and beef short ribs, plus chicken, prime rib, pork loin, chopped beef, sausage, turkey, and even rainbow trout. Our favorite, though, was the brisket, tender and cooked to smoky perfection. Complement the meats with some of Rudy's sauce. It's so good that fans from around the state now have the dark concoction shipped to their homes (see Appendix B for details).

TEXAS OLD FASHION BAR-B-QUE
1023 Austin Hwy. (210) 826-0800
Cash. Order/pick up. Catering.

Located down the street from the Bun 'n Barrel, this typical Texas barbecue joint is nothing fancy and not near as atmospheric as its neighbor. It does serve up plenty of good brisket, chicken, and lots of ribs, though: beef, baby back, spare, and even slabs of pork ribs and lamb ribs. Save room for the sweet potato pie, an unusual treat.

TOM'S RIBS
13323 Nacogdoches Rd. (210) 654-RIBS
Cash/credit. Table service/take out.

When San Antonians go out for a nice family barbecue dinner, many head to Tom's Ribs, north of the 410 loop. This eatery is plusher than most, with a bar, carpet, booth and table service, and, unfortunately, higher prices than those found in most pits. However, when you're looking for a nice sit-down restaurant where you can wrap your hands around a baby back rib and clean up on premoistened towelettes when you're finished, this is the place.

Tom's mascot is a lip lickin' pig with a bib around his neck and silverware in each front foot. Be prepared to feel like that pig when you place an order for a slab of baby back pork ribs. The waitress will robe you up with a plastic bib (sporting none other than the Tom's pig). Chicken and sausage are available as well, served up with two side dishes from a list of a dozen. Besides the usual, diners can feast on Italian green beans and new potatoes, hot buttered carrots, sweet potatoes, or Tom's own Whiskey River Baked Beans.

The waitstaff wears T-shirts proclaiming "Praise the Pig and Pass the Napkins." With ribs this good, what's a little mess?

TONY ROMA'S—A PLACE FOR RIBS
9921 I-10 W. (210) 432-7427
Cash/credit. Table service.
River Center Mall, 849 E. Commerce. (210) 225-7662
Cash/credit. Table service.

Like all Tony Roma locations in the chain, the San Antonio locations are pleasant, paneled restaurants with a warm, dark decor featuring historic photos of Tony Roma. We like the River Center Mall location, though. Ask for an outdoor table overlooking the River Walk and watch the river taxis filled with San Antonio visitors make their turn around in the mall. (For a full review of Tony Roma's, see the Dallas listings in the "On the Road" section.)

SAN MARCOS

The home of Southwest Texas State University, San Marcos is located 30 minutes south of Austin on busy Interstate 35. Every summer, this college town hosts Chilympiad, the world's largest chili cook-off.

FUSCHAK'S PIT BAR-B-Q
920 Hwy. 80. (512) 353-2712
Cash. Order/pick up/carry out/drive through.

This sit-down restaurant, located on the east side of I-35, takes the best Texas cuisines—Tex-Mex and barbecue—and combines them into one. The Bar-Burrito, one of the best bargains on the menu, is also one of the most popular items. It starts with a flour tortilla filled with refried beans, cheddar cheese, and hot sauce, then on comes beef brisket and barbecue sauce for a true Texas meal. Fuschak's also does a barbecue twist on another Tex-Mex favorite: the fajita. The San Marcos version presents fajita meat, barbecue sauce, hot sauce, and guacamole rolled in a tortilla.

There are plenty of traditional dishes, too. Brisket, sausage, pork ribs, and chicken are served with a choice of country-style french fries, tangy mustard-spiced potato salad, coleslaw, beans, and banana pudding.

Diners can enjoy a large dining room, decorated with antique farm implements, a large fireplace, and even a photo of Earl Campbell during his Longhorn football days. For those on the move, there's drive-through service and walk-in take out service.

SCHERTZ

For years, folks slowed down as they passed through Schertz and the neighboring community of Selma for one reason: to avoid the interstate speed trap. Now, thanks to an old-fashioned barbecue joint, there's an even better reason to slow down on I-35 just north of San Antonio.

GARDEN RIDGE SMOKEHOUSE
17967 I-35 N. (210) 651-6606

Cash. Order/pick up.

The easiest way to find this pit is to look for Garden Ridge Pottery, a megashop that attracts visitors from all over the state. Look for the orange metal buildings and the acres of cars and buses, then check out the smoke at the corner of the parking lot. That's the Garden Ridge Smokehouse, and it draws its own share of visitors.

Although it's located next to one of Texas's largest stores, don't look for a slick shopping center eatery here. This is a genuine Texas smokehouse, from the picnic tables out front to the sawdust-covered floor in the dining room to the screened porch behind the kitchen. And the product is genuine as well. Order the sausage, a chunky, peppery blend that's made by the City Market in Schulenburg. We ordered a sausage wrap, with a generous length of sausage wrapped in a flour tortilla. You can also have sausage on a stick, a sausage sandwich, or a plate served with potato salad or slaw and pintos.

Garden Ridge also sells sliced brisket, smoked chicken, and pork ribs, all slow cooked over mesquite.

SCHULENBURG

This hamlet is tucked beneath an overpass of busy I-10. It's well worth the time to exit the interstate, however, to dine in one of two excellent restaurants or shop for barbecue-related gifts.

GUENTERT'S BARBECUE RESTAURANT
AND COUNTRY MEAT MARKET
TX 77 (1/2 mile north of I-10). (409) 743-4688

Cash/credit. Order/pick up. Catering.

Some folks believe you can find a good restaurant by following the truckers. Hungry 18-wheeler drivers know the best pit stops on the road. If that's true, then Guentert's is a sure thing. Trucks fill the parking lot starting early in the morning as drivers arrive for breakfast. Barbecue is the order of the day—chicken, pork ribs, sausage (a beef and pork combo), brisket, and pork—served with hot potatoes or potato salad, pinto beans, coleslaw, and homemade bread.

Along with the dining room, there's a meat market out front. "Curtis had a meat processing plant and decided to get into the food line," explains Mrs. Guentert. The market sells fresh home-killed, corn-fed beef, plus an assortment of cuts and sausages.

OAKRIDGE SMOKEHOUSE RESTAURANT
I-10 and TX 77. (409) 743-3372

Cash/credit. Table service.

Like a fun house in an Ozark amusement park, this building is constructed to look like it's on the verge of collapse. Windows hang at odd angles to the doors, and the foundation looks like it has weathered an earthquake. But the Oakridge Smokehouse is far from its demise. In business nearly half a century, this family-owned company keeps churning out barbecue and sausage to please travelers on busy I-10 and mail order customers around the country (see Appendix B).

You enter through a huge gift shop stocked with Texas products and food items. The restaurant beyond is large and full service, offering sausage, pork ribs, and brisket, all served up with a side of sauerkraut.

SEWARD JUNCTION

Seward Junction is literally just a wide place in the road. Located at the intersection of US 183 and TX 29 north of Leander, there's not much to see here. But who needs to see anything when you can smell the scent of a smoky pit?

DONN'S PIT STOP BAR-B-QUE
US 183 and TX 29. (512) 778-6171

Cash. Order/pick up.

Everybody has their local barbecue joint, the place they run by to pick up a family pack when company's coming or they just don't feel like cooking. Donn's is one of our regular stops. Every so often, we have to have a Donn's fix. A taste of that lean brisket, with a crusty topping covering a rosy smoky ring. A bite of moist chicken or ham. A link of spicy sausage.

As much as we like the meats, the side dishes are good enough to be a meal in themselves. Donn's beans are different from any others we've tried (and that's saying a lot). Owners Don and Myra Subocz add ground sausage to the pot, imparting a spicy taste to what many restaurants serve as an all-too-often bland side dish. We could make a meal with a bowl of these beans and some Mrs. Baird's spongy white bread. The potato salad is also a step above the usual, a crunchy mixture of finely chopped potatoes, onions, and pickles.

We always get our order to go, but you can eat outside on a shaded picnic table if you like. Flaps fend off bad weather.

SMITHVILLE

Located on the Colorado River, this small town east of Austin was once a riverboat stop. Today it's the modern version: a stop for travelers between Austin and Houston on busy TX 71. To reach Smithville from Austin, take TX 71 southeast for 42 miles.

CHARLES' BAR-B-QUE
100 Main St. (512) 237-3317

Cash. Order/pick up. Catering.

This pit in downtown Smithville near the railroad tracks was once part of the Mikeska kingdom, the throne from where Mike Mikeska ruled. Today brother Mike is retired and the joint is owned by Charles Ebner, but he still churns out plenty of spicy barbecue in a place that's right out of the BBQ textbook—from the squeaky screen door and the smoky windows to the ceiling fans and the bottles of unnamed liquid atop vinyl-clothed tables. The plywood floor and white plaster walls finish off the atmosphere.

Like any true Texas joint, this one has plenty of meats: brisket, ham, chicken, sausage, pork, pork ribs, and even mutton. They're all served up with coleslaw, potato salad, and beans. Liven up those taste buds with a squirt from the ketchup bottles holding a witch's brew of vinegar and spices—the combination is potent enough to clear up your sinuses.

ZIMMERHANZEL'S BAR-B-QUE
TX 95. (512) 237-4244
Cash. Cafeteria style.

This popular Smithville pit is always filled with locals, sometimes lined up from the counter all the way to the door. Taste the pit's product and you'll see why. Located in a bright orange metal building, you can't miss Zimmerhanzel's. There's not much atmosphere here, but the barbecue makes up for any blandness in decor. Order brisket, pork ribs, chicken, or sausage, served with beans, potato salad, macaroni salad, or coleslaw. We were especially fond of the tender, succulent brisket and the spicy sausage.

TAYLOR

Taylor calls itself "The Barbecue Capital of the World." And why not? With three excellent barbecue restaurants and one of the biggest cook-offs in the state, Taylor is certainly a smokin' place. To get here, head north from Austin on I-35 to Round Rock. Turn east on US 79 and then continue for 17 miles.

LOUIS MUELLER BARBEQUE
206 W. Second St. (512) 352-6206
Cash. Order/pick up.

Louis Mueller's is small-town Texas like most people only get to see in the movies. First, there's the clientele. You'll see folks from every walk of Taylor life here, from the college boys to the car mechanics to the cotton farmers. Then there's the setting. Taylor is tucked between cotton fields, forgotten by the interstate highway system, so you won't see nearly as much change in this town as in some. The downtown looks just about the same as it has for generations. This isn't a small town where people come to shop for antiques or search through boutiques; they come here to sell their cotton crop and buy farm machinery.

And finally there's the building. Louis Mueller's is housed in the most authentic barbecue joint in Texas, from the slamming screen door to the smoke-covered walls to the giant fans that provide the only cool breeze on a hot summer day. The walls here were once painted a dark green; today they look like someone has attempted to antique them with black paint. That's no black paint, though—it's smoke, and plenty of it. Smoke streaks the walls, the ceiling two stories above, the free calendars hanging around the place, and the corkboard full of business cards (they're so coated with smoke they look like they were all made from brown grocery sacks).

Of course the real measure of a genuine barbecue joint is its product, and Louis Mueller's is as good as you can get. It's tender, it's flavorful, it's consistent, and it's cheap. Not one to waste money on fancy gimmicks like plates, Mueller's serves up meat on a piece of white butcher paper. You can still get a helping of pork ribs with a side order for less than $3.

And don't look for fancy menus here either. There's a movable letter board on one wall with the offerings. (A few letters are missing, but everyone knows what Louis Mueller's has, and everyone knows what they want.) You can pick from brisket, served regular or extra lean, sausage, pork ribs, chopped beef, or steak. Grab a tray, step up to the counter, and the cook will carve off a slice of meat to satisfy your own proportions. For a side dish, you can order coleslaw, beans, or potato salad, the latter a mix of mashed potatoes spiced with onion and celery.

The meats are served with a Styrofoam cup of sauce on the side. Mueller's sauce is different than others; it consists of a tomatoey broth spiced with onions and lots of black pepper. (We liked the sauce as a dip for the white bread slices you get with your order.) The meats, seasoned with a dry rub, are spicy without the sauce, but for real fire eaters there's a vinegar and chili pepper sauce bottle on every table. Don't look for a label on the bottle— this is a homemade concoction. One sprinkle on your meat, though, and you'll know that this is hot sauce.

RUDY MIKESKA'S BAR-B-Q INC.
300 W. Second St. (512) 352-5561 or (800) 962-5706
Cash/credit. Cafeteria style. Catering.

During his lifetime, Rudy Mikeska was the dean of Texas pitmasters. If there was a political function to be held, whether it was a policemen's fundraiser or a governor's inauguration, Rudy Mikeska and his barbecue meats were there. In Texas the Mikeska name is synonymous with barbecue, thanks to Rudy and his brothers, Maurice, Clem, Jerry, Mike, and Louis. Each man founded his own barbecue restaurant, spread throughout the state in Taylor,

Temple, El Campo, Columbus, and Smithville (that location has now changed hands). This accomplishment made *Texas Monthly* proclaim the brothers "The First Family of Texas Barbecue." Their restaurants were no chain of pits, however; each man had his own preferences and his own way of preparing barbecue. "We're a very close family," explains CEO Tim Mikeska, "but we all do things a little different." You may visit all the locations, but don't expect to see identical menus or taste identical food.

Rudy died in 1989, but he left a legacy of legendary barbecue that his children Tim and Mopsie continue. Step inside the bright red building in downtown Taylor and have a look around at the dozens of pictures of Rudy Mikeska and the wheelers and dealers of Texas. You'll find photos of politicians on every level here, posing beside Mikeska at various events he catered. You'll also see plaques of appreciation and awards from barbecue contests like Taylor's International Barbecue Cookoff.

But judge for yourself. Step up to the cafeteria line and order up a plate. You'll find lamb ribs on the menu, but the popular favorites are brisket, sausage, and pork ribs. The sausage is made using Mikeska's own recipe, thin links full of peppery fire. The potato salad is creamy and chunky, a good way to cool the burn. The pinto beans are flavorful but not too spicy. You can also have fried potatoes and onions, and some homemade white bread.

Save room for the banana pudding. It is chock full of banana slices and vanilla wafers, a real tribute to the favorite dessert in all barbecue joints and to the man who made this one a legend.

TAYLOR CAFE
101 N. Main. (512) 352-8475
Cash. Counter and table service.

You really shouldn't call this place a cafe. Or a restaurant. Or a diner. It's a dive. A joint. A hole in the wall. And that's what makes a trip to the Taylor Cafe so much fun. That and a plate topped with some great barbecue.
The Taylor Cafe would be easy to miss, located beneath an overpass by the railyard. But thanks to the red exterior, the hand-lettered "Taylor Cafe" sign, and the row of cars around the joint, you can't miss this barbecue hot spot. And, if it's lunchtime, just look for the police cars. Seems the Taylor Police Department hangs out here, at a table around past the pool table and the jukebox.

Inside, the Taylor Cafe is dark and filled with the sound of ceiling fans and conversation. There's no air conditioning here, just a screen door that pops shut as another local enters to place his usual lunch order. You can have your lunch at the counter or at one of the mismatched tables, but wherever you sit, have a look around. This is the hole-in-the-wall look that others try to imitate but never get quite right. The ceiling is plywood, the walls are unpainted chipboard, the decorations are neon beer signs and mounted deer trophies.

Pickin's are slim here. The menu is simple and posted on the wall by the counter. You can have a brisket or sausage plate or a mixed plate with some of both. The brisket is lean and full of smoky flavor, good enough to make Taylor proud. The sausage is coarsely ground and full of peppery taste. Plates come with a dollop of tangy potato salad and pintos plus a basket of white bread and some soda crackers. There's no barbecue sauce served here, just unlabeled bottles on the tables filled with a red peppery liquid that will perk up any taste bud.

You can also opt for the sliced beef or chopped beef sandwich. (Go for the sliced beef; the chopped beef is too fatty for most tastes.) Pork ribs and turkey sausage are also for sale by the pound.

Wash it all down with a cold beer or iced tea. The tea is served sweetened, and you get a whole pitcher at your table.

TEMPLE

Located between Austin and Waco on Interstate 35, Temple is home to one of the Mikeska clan barbecue joints. It's only a stone (or a rib bone's) throw from the interstate.

CLEM MIKESKA'S BAR-B-Q
1217 S. 57th (57th at Ave. M). (817) 778-5481
or (800) 344-4699

Cash / credit. Cafeteria style / take out / drive through. Catering.

You can't miss Clem Mikeska's as you drive north on Interstate 35 through Temple—there's a cow on the roof. That bovine is a clue to the meats that wait within this dark red building. Clem's advertises premium beef, and that's no joke. We found that the brisket here was some of the best we've had, and that's covering a lot of ground. It's tender and lean, without a tough or stringy spot on it.

Folks have been enjoying this comfortable but unassuming restaurant since 1965. Clem is one of the Mikeska brothers famed throughout Texas for their barbecue restaurants. Each brother runs his restaurant a little differently, though, so you've got a good excuse to visit the whole lot of them. Besides brisket, Clem's serves homemade beef sausage (it's excellent—spicy but not too hot), pork ribs, and chicken, with green beans, brown beans, hot buttered potatoes, potato salad, or coleslaw on the side. We opted for the mustard-based chunky potato salad and the beans tinged slightly red with spice. Grab a few slices of homemade bread as you go through the line to sop up the last drops of barbecue sauce from your plate.

If you can forgo the temptation of stuffing yourself with barbecue, save room for dessert. Clem's has peach cobbler and banana pudding, chock full of vanilla wafers.

You'll find a mix of Temple folks in Clem's, from auto mechanics to business and medical professionals. The dining room, filled with booths and tables done in red-and-white checked tablecloths, is packed at noon. Like the dining rooms at other restaurants owned by the Mikeska family, this one is filled with photos of Texas dignitaries and family members as well as wildlife trophies. A hammerhead shark looms overhead as you pay, and a buffalo gazes at diners from the back of the room.

VOLENTE

Tiny Volente is located northwest of Austin on the shores of Lake Travis. To reach this village, travel north of Austin on US 183 to RR 620. Turn west and continue to the intersection of RR 2769, then turn right. Volente is located at the intersection of RR 2769 and Lime Creek Road.

VOLENTE BAR-B-QUE INC.
15920 RR 2769. (512) 219-1136

Cash. Order/pick up. Catering.

The fishing village is filled with boat docks, marinas, and lakeside homes. In such a setting, you wouldn't be surprised to see a first-class fish restaurant— but barbecue? Well, here it is. Partners Don Hopkins and Fletcher Jamar started this lakeside smokehouse a few years ago. "My partner sells barbecue pits, and we've been friends for years. We decided one day to get together and open this up," says Don. "We're way out on Lake Travis, and you've got to know we're here to find us."

It's worth the winding drive from Austin to find this eatery (usually open only Saturday, Sunday, and Monday) that specializes in pork ribs, ones that have won barbecue cook-offs. Hopkins and Jamar cook the ribs over oak and season them with secret spices. Along with those tender pork ribs, look for beef brisket and Smoky Denmarks sausage, an Austin product. You can have your sausage on a plate with the side dish trimmings or wrapped up in white bread or a flour tortilla.

When you order those side dishes, don't miss the potato salad or the beans. Disguised as regular pintos, these beans are well seasoned and spiced with peppers, making them good enough to be a meal in themselves.

PART TWO
ON THE ROAD

Much of the barbecue in Texas is found in the central region, but you'll find tasty 'que in every corner of the Lone Star State. Without compiling an encyclopedia, though, it's impossible to cover the thousands of pits smoking across the state. Every community has a barbecue place, and every place has its die-hard fans who will swear that it's the best. And maybe it is.

Since our waistlines wouldn't permit us to visit every pit, we chose some of the state's best known joints outside the Barbecue Belt. When you're on the road again, here are a few suggestions for finding a good barbecue plate and good pit atmosphere, whether you're on the Mexican border, the Gulf beach, or the streets of the Big D.

RESTAURANT LISTING

DALLAS

Perhaps more than any other Texas city, Dallas seems quite familiar to folks throughout the country. It's the Big D, the home of the Dallas Cowboys, the city where President Kennedy was assassinated, J.R.'s hometown. What you may not know, though, is that this city is smokin'. As cosmopolitan as Dallas is, residents all across the Metroplex enjoy wrapping their hands around a dripping rib as much as diners do in the tiniest of Texas hamlets.

DICK'S LAST RESORT
Ross at Record (West End). (214) 747-0001

Cash / credit. Table service / take out.

Dick's is located in the trendy West End historic district, a collection of hip shops and tony night clubs set in a remodeled, turn-of-the-century cookie and candy factory. This Dick's location is the home base of the popular chain, which has a location in San Antonio and several out of state. What makes Dick's special, besides some terrific food, is its wacky atmosphere. From a wise-cracking waitstaff to restrooms sporting fluorescent condom machines to matchbooks featuring topless women, this restaurant is lewd, crude, and proud of it.

Dick's offers both pork and beef ribs (the largest we've had), barbecue chicken, and barbecue shrimp. It's all served up in small tin buckets on a tablecloth of white butcher paper. The pork ribs are fall-off-the-bone tender, and the beef ribs are meaty and smoky. The shrimp are jumbo, served three on a skewer and slathered with sauce. Entrees are served with a bucket of french fries and bread.

Save room for the desserts: Mississippi mud pie, cheesecake, and that Texas favorite, pecan pie.

PEGGY SUE BBQ
6600 Snider Plaza. (214) 987-9188

Cash / credit. Table service / take out.

Peggy Sue's barbecue is not the best known in Dallas, and it's not the oldest. But age and popularity can't guarantee what this joint promises: some of the best barbecue in the Big D, plus great atmosphere. Diners here chow down in a sea of '50s memorabilia, from hand-tinted photos to cowboy hats suspended from the ceiling. All the Happy Days kitsch is just whipped cream on a prize-winning sundae of barbecue. We tried the baby back ribs, peppery and full of smoky wonder, spare ribs seasoned with a secret rub, chicken whose pink depths hinted at its trial by fire, and oak-smoked brisket, served lean and sliced the thickness of a few Neiman Marcus credit cards. Peggy Sue's also boasts turkey, Polish kielbasa sausage, and ham, offerings we had to save for another day.

You can begin your meal with BBQuesadillas, a variation of that Tex-Mex favorite made with chopped brisket. Save room, though, for the generous portions on the plates, served with two side dishes: pinto beans, squash casserole, spinach, french fries, green beans, carrots, slaw, broccoli, onion rings, corn, or potato salad. The latter is a refreshing twist on an old favorite, a melding of cubed potatoes, celery, bacon, and egg.

Peggy Sue's has not one but two barbecue sauces, a mild tomatoey mixture served in squirt containers and a peppery mix offered in an open-necked bottle. The hotter sauce is a definite winner, a combination of wickedly hot black pepper and some slightly sweet spices. Mix it with the pintos for an above-average side dish. If you've saved room, follow the meal with a fried pie, peach cobbler, or that '50s favorite, a root beer float.

RAYMOND'S BAR-B-Q
10920 Garland Rd. (214) 327-5800
Cash / credit. Cafeteria style / take out. Catering.

Some things in life don't change, like Raymond's Bar-B-Que. Even though Dallas has seen lots of change and high tech progress, Raymond's still does what it does best: turn out tasty barbecue. Since Raymond Erwin started his joint in 1954, this pit has been smoking meats for the folks in east-central Dallas.

The 120-seat dining room is like a poster for the 1950s, dotted with butter-colored vinyl booths. Chile ristas hang from the lights, adding a Southwest flair to the diner. Raymond's specialities are brisket, lean and tender, and sausage, a combination of pork and beef. You can also order up pork ribs, turkey, or ham, all served with beans, potato salad, and coleslaw.

SONNY BRYAN'S SMOKEHOUSE
2202 Inwood Rd. (214) 357-7120
Cash / credit. Order / pick up. Catering.

302 N. Market (West End). (214) 744-1610
Cash / credit. Order / pick up / table service at dinner.

325 N. St. Paul. (214) 979-0102
Cash. Order / pick up.

Plaza of the Americas Hotel (San Jacinto and Pearl Sts.). (214) 871-2097
Cash. Order / pick up.

4701 Frankford at Tollway. (214) 447-0102
Cash / credit. Order / pick up / table service at dinner.

Galleria Mall (Macy's Food Court). (214) 851-5131
Cash. Order / pick up.

The fame of Sonny Bryan's barbecue has spread far beyond the Dallas area. For out-of-towners as well as thousands of loyal locals, Sonny Bryan's is barbecue in the Big D. For one thing, this place looks like a barbecue joint should. Small and decidedly no frills, it seems to have been transported from a small Texas town and dropped among the freeways and high-rises. Located just northwest of the downtown area, Sonny Bryan's is a lunchtime legend; its tiny dining area equipped with benches and old school desks is often thronged with both white and blue collar fans.

The menu, likewise, is no frills. Ribs dripping with a slightly sweet sauce, smoked Eckridge sausage, or sliced beef on a bun are the staples. Or order any meat dinner-style by adding coleslaw, barbecue beans, and a hamburger bun that serves as bread. Huge onion rings and french fries are other popular menu items. All meals are served on paper plates (good heavy ones that can take the weight in case you can't find a seat), with real metal flatware and, incredibly, crisp white cloth napkins that seem as out of place in this joint as a tuxedo in a pool hall.

About the only thing decorative about Sonny Bryan's is a horseshoe that has hung over the counter for as long as this place has been part of Dallas's urban mythology. Who says you can't buy good luck? While you're in line, check out the newspaper clippings featuring this popular eatery, including one describing a visit from Julia Child. The Oak Ridge Boys' autographed photos also recall other happy customers.

Sonny Bryan's has grown so successful that today Dallas is dotted with them. The other locations offer a few additional dishes not served at the original Inwood Road pit, including chicken-fried steak, chicken-fried chicken, salads, chicken wings, hamburgers, and baked potatoes.

TONY ROMA'S—A PLACE FOR RIBS
10945 Composite Blvd. (214) 353-0104
Cash/credit. Table service.
310 Market (West End). (214) 748-6959
Cash/credit. Table service.

Tony Roma's is not a native Texas enterprise. However, a few foods, like chicken-fried steak, corn bread, and pecan pie, seem to improve when they cross the state line. Maybe it's the Texas air. Maybe it's the water. Whatever the reason, this import can be declared a genuine Texan as far as we're concerned because their ribs do the Lone Star State proud. Tony Roma's began in Miami, Florida, in 1972, serving up baby back ribs that drew diners from near and far. In January 1976, Clint Murchison, Jr., then owner of the Dallas Cowboys, was in Miami for the Super Bowl and dined on Tony's specialty. Murchison liked those ribs so much he bought the franchise rights to the place, and today there are Tony Roma's around the country as well as in the Bahamas, Canada, England, Grand Cayman, Guam, Hong Kong, Japan, Mexico, Puerto Rico, and Singapore.

Start off with a loaf of onion rings, golden batter dipped rings compressed into a brick shape. Save room for the ribs, though. Our favorite are the Original Baby Backs, fall-apart-in-your-mouth tender and basted with Tony Roma's original sauce (you can buy a bottle and try your luck on your home pit). The ragin' Cajun-style ribs are also mighty tasty, basted with a secret mix of spices that makes them a little more flavorful than the original. There's also the Carolina Honeys, a pork rib coated with a honey and molasses sauce. We'd also recommend the St. Louis–style pork spare ribs and the jumbo Bountiful Beef ribs, which were meaty but a little tough. Can't decide? Do what we did and order the sampler plate.

If someone in your party is not in a rib mood, the menu also offers barbecued chicken and grilled sausage sandwiches, plus several club sandwiches and burgers.

Along with these Dallas locations, there are two other Tony Roma's in the vicinity: Addison and Mesquite.

EL PASO

Perched at the western tip of Texas, El Paso is a blend of many cuisines: Mexican, Tex-Mex, and New Mexican. But barbecue? You bet your brisket. The city on the banks of the Rio Grande is home to some smokin' joints that offer mighty tasty meats and an El Paso specialty: pineapple coleslaw. A sweet-and-sour blend, this combination is good enough to make typical slaw seem downright boring. The city is also home to the El Paso Chile Company, one of the state's biggest distributors of specialty sauces and marinades (see Appendix B: Barbecue Gifts and Products).

BILL PARK'S BAR-B-Q
3130 Gateway E. between Piedras and Copia.
(915) 542-0960

Cash / credit. Table service. Catering.

Bill Park's may be located at the western end of Texas, but this is Deep South cooking at its best. Corn bread muffins (or johnnycakes drizzled with maple syrup when the corn bread supply has been depleted), sweet potato pie, catfish plates, a lunch special of pork feet and neck bones, and sides including mixed greens and okra and tomatoes make this a Dixie restaurant where Spanish is heard as often as English.

And the main dish is good old-fashioned 'que: chicken, beef ribs, brisket, pork ribs, sliced pork, ham, sausage, and hot links. We were particularly fond of the brisket, tender and sliced thin and lean. The sausage was peppery and chunky, served cut down to the center with a ladleful of dark, almost brown, sauce to add a little heat.

The sides are varied, from pintos to potato salad. The chunky potato salad is mighty flavorful, and the coleslaw is some of El Paso's finest, spiked with chunks of pineapple.

There are two dining rooms at Bill Park's with large aquariums to liven the decor. And you can't miss the signs, fluorescent displays with advice like "Eat out—the wife you save may be your own."

JAXON'S RESTAURANT
1135 Airway at Viscount. (915) 778-9696

Cash / credit. Table service.

4799 N. Mesa. (915) 544-1188

Cash / credit. Table service.

When El Paso residents are ready to celebrate a special event or to meet for a power lunch, they head to Jaxon's. This upscale restaurant recognizes both El Paso history and El Paso cuisine, a term that encompasses from chicken-fried steak to Tampico steak to fajitas and quesadillas. The walls of Jaxon's on Airway are filled with over 500 photos of the city and decorated with murals depicting the history of El Paso.

But barbecue lovers know there's another reason to come to Jaxon's: the Santa Barbara Beef®. "The meat is the centerpiece," says Jaxon's general manager Mike Coulter. "We use grilled sirloin. It's milder and leaner than brisket." The cut is called tri-tip, the upper part of the flank of a side of beef near the ribs. This special dish is served with barbecue sauce on the side and a choice of fries, baked potato, or rice pilaf. Take a few moments to note the barbecue sauce. It's flavorful and a little different, possibly because of its two special ingredients: honey and coffee.

Besides the Santa Barbara Beef, look for baby back ribs, meaty, juicy ribs served up with that El Paso specialty: pineapple coleslaw.

SMITTY'S PIT BAR-B-QUE
6219 Airport Rd. at Montana St. (915) 772-5876
Cash/credit. Table service/take out. Catering.

From 1955 to 1976, Smitty's was the pit of Mr. Smith. Since that bicentennial year, though, Smitty's has been smokin' with the meats of Irene and Heriberto Payan and their son, Eddie, producing some of El Paso's best loved barbecue using the original recipes. Located just down the road from the El Paso International Airport, it's been the first stop for many a traveler to this West Texas city. And with good reason. Tender briskets, marinated 24 to 48 hours before cooking, are packed with all the smoky flavor of Smitty's pit, an enormous brick contraption that cooks 240 pounds at a time. The barbecued beans are cooked in the pit as well.

Deciding where to sit here is easy: The restaurant has just a counter and booths, nary a table in sight. The hard part of your visit is deciding what to order: brisket, corned beef, ham, turkey, pork, hot links, or pork or beef ribs. We had the brisket, tender and flavorful, the hot links, a combination of pork and beef made here in the restaurant, and the pork ribs, some of the best we've enjoyed. We also tried the corned beef, and found this smoky creation one of our favorites, with a firmer consistency than brisket and filled with a wonderful combination of flavors. The meats are offered with two kinds of barbecue sauce, a mild version and a spicy edition that we loved. A small dish of peppers also arrives with every meal.

All the plates here include coleslaw, barbecued beans, and a Smitty specialty: German fried potatoes (see the recipe in on p. 131).

SMOKEY'S PIT STOP
1346 Lee Trevino. (915) 596-6332

Cash/credit. Cafeteria style. Catering.

9100 Viscount. (915) 592-3141

Cash/credit. Cafeteria style. Catering.

Grab a tray and start down the line. Smokey's lays an entire spread of good barbecue before you, ready to select. And that's the hard part. There are plenty of meats: brisket, pork loin, ham, sausage, chicken, fajita meat, turkey, beef and pork ribs, and even baby backs.

We didn't have the chance to try all the smoke-filled offerings, but what we did try was very good. Don't overlook the burrito plates—tortillas the size of Frisbees packed with chopped beef and sauce, and served with a choice of potato salad, coleslaw, chili beans, chips, red beans and rice, or corn on the cob. The potato salad and coleslaw are excellent, but don't miss the chili beans. These are some of our favorites, zesty beans mixed with shredded meat and peppers that are good enough to make a meal in themselves.

FORT WORTH

Fort Worth is Dallas's country cousin. Here's a town where you can go to the Stockyards and watch a rodeo, then belly up to a bar in historic Sundance Square. With its Western heritage, it's not surprising that Fort Worth is home to a wildly popular barbecue joint. Ask any Fort Worth citizen where to go for smoky meats, and you'll hear one name: Angelo's.

ANGELO'S
2533 White Settlement Rd. (817) 332-0357

Cash. Table service after 3 p.m.

Angelo's sounds like the kind of place where you'd go for lasagna and breadsticks instead of longnecks and barbecue. But make no mistake, this is a real Texas barbecue joint all right. Named for owner Angelo George, the restaurant serves up Fort Worth's favorite smoked delights in a family atmosphere.

For lunch, there are sandwiches and side orders only. Order beans, creamy potato salad, or coleslaw to accompany a tasty sandwich stuffed with tender brisket. But come after three in the afternoon for Angelo's full show.

After that magic hour, you'll have table service plus a choice of plates: brisket or pork ribs or a combination of the two. Both are about as good as you can get, so you can't go wrong. The brisket is tender and shot through with smoky taste, and the ribs are crusty and coated with secret spices. It's all served up with a tomatoey sauce that adds just the right amount of spice to an already flavorful meal.

Mere lasagna could never satisfy so well.

GLEN ROSE

Tiny Glen Rose is located southwest of Fort Worth, a community best known for its dinosaur tracks, nuclear power plant, and African wildlife conservation park. It's also home to some mighty tasty barbecue.

DEBBIE'S
US 67. (817) 897-4399
Cash. Table service.

Debbie's is housed in a prefab building next door to Hammond's. While the neighboring pit draws huge dinner crowds, Debbie's packs 'em in for breakfast and lunch only. Besides one of the best (and largest) breakfasts we've ever eaten, Debbie's also offers plenty of barbecue. Plates are served with potato salad, slaw, and beans. Save room for the cobbler!

HAMMOND'S BAR-B-Q
US 67. (817) 897-2324
Cash / credit. Table service.

"Whoa, here Tis," says the sign at Hammond's Bar-B-Q. And, indeed, here it is. Tender brisket, fall-off-the-bone tender ribs, and slightly spicy sausage, all served up in a genuine barbecue joint atmosphere, complete with a sawdust-covered floor.

We enjoyed plates of thinly sliced brisket and spicy ribs, plus a sausage sandwich. Unlike central Texas hot links, the sausage here is fat 'n sassy, a much larger concoction than many joints serve. Hammond's promises "country cooking all the way." Check out that promise with the mustard-based potato salad or finely chopped coleslaw. The plates are served with a *molcajete* of barbecue sauce and that Lone Star favorite, Texas toast. These fat slabs of white bread are tossed in the pit for a few minutes, a fine complement to any meal and good enough to eat like cake.

Hammond's doesn't serve alcoholic beverages during the annual run of "The Promise." This religious drama plays in Glen Rose every fall and summer and draws crowds from around the South. When the production ceases, you can buy beer in a tin building next door called the "Galvanized Palace" and carry your beverage into the restaurant.

HOUSTON

Houston is known as the sprawling exuberant capital of the "oil bidness" or as NASA's Mission Control in space exploration, or for its huge seaport, located 50 miles from the coast. Houston's population is composed of ethnic groups from all over the world. This diversity is reflected in its generous selection of ethnic restaurants, a smorgasbord of international cuisines. This array also includes delicacies from right around the corner, like, well, barbecue. After all, Houston is also a major center for another big Texas "bidness"—ranching.

BILLY BLUES
6025 Richmond Ave. (713) 266-9294
Cash/credit. Table service.

Pecan-smoked barbecue is the order of the day at this popular restaurant, part of a San Antonio–based chain. What makes this location stand out is the Smokesax, a 63-foot statue that's the creation of artist Bob "Daddy-O" Wade. Commemorating Houston's history of R&B, this sculpture holds the distinction as the world's largest saxophone sculpture. The artwork is built on a Volkswagen chassis and sports a surfboard for a reed. Since, after all, this is a barbecue joint, the sculpture blows real smoke. (For details on this chain, see the San Antonio portion of "Along the Barbecue Belt.")

COUNTY LINE
13850 Cutten Rd. (1 mile north of FM 1960). (713) 537-2454
Cash/credit. Table service.
6159 Westheimer near Fountainview. (713) 784-8777
Cash/credit. Table service.

Part of a popular Austin-based chain, these Houston locations offer the same unbeatable family-style dining. The Cutten Road restaurant, set among tall pines in the northwest part of the city, has two specialties of the house: smoked prime rib and smoked pork tenderloin. This location is closed

Mondays and Tuesdays. The Westheimer restaurant, near the Galleria mall, is open daily. (For a full rundown on these restaurants, see the Austin portion of "Along the Barbecue Belt.")

GOODE COMPANY BARBEQUE
5109 Kirby (between Southwest Fwy. and Bissonet).
(713) 522-2530

Cash/credit. Cafeteria style. Catering.

How good is Goode? Find out for yourself. Step in line in this building constructed to look like an old-fashioned barn and order up some tasty brisket. Or crusty pork ribs. Or moist chicken or ham. Or for something different, smoked duck. Duck? In a Texas barbecue joint? What is this world coming to?

Have no fear. Even though Goode serves duck (not to mention Texas wines), there's no hint at snootiness in this joint. Just have a look around at the cordwood stacked outside, the neon beer signs, and even the armadillo decorating the place. But decor does not a barbecue joint make, product does. And one taste of the Goode meats will tell you that this isn't just good, it's goode.

Besides some delicious barbecue, there's also a full offering of side dishes here, far more exotic than the typical beans and potato salad. Look for jalapeño-laced pintos and, our favorite, a cheesy jalapeño bread.

LULING CITY MARKET BAR-B-Q RESTAURANT
AND BAR
4726 Richmond. (713) 871-1903

Cash/credit. Cafeteria style.

If you liked the Luling City Market in Luling, then don't miss this location. The owners aren't related, but the restaurants have the same cooks, concept, and recipes, giving Houston a taste of small-town barbecue the way it ought to be.

As at the old hometown meat markets, you order up brisket and pork ribs by weight here. We were smitten with both the smoky, moist brisket and the crunchy, spicy ribs, both served up with coleslaw, beans, and potato salad. We didn't get to try the beef links and chicken, but if they come close to the other items, they're sure winners.

LUTHER'S BAR-B-Q
1100 Smith. (713) 759-0018
Cash / credit. Cafeteria style. Catering.

Luther's is one of the best known barbecue joints in Houston because it's everywhere. Locations dot the city like beans in a pot, feeding the hungry masses on their lunch breaks. It's not surprising then that when the 1990 Economic Summit came to Houston, Luther's was chosen to feed the 5,000 participants. The busy pit smoked up an astounding three and a half tons of brisket, sausage, chicken, and ribs, served with a ton and a half of coleslaw, potato salad, and beans. It was all washed down with 650 gallons of iced tea and lemonade.

That was certainly a Texas-sized order, but Luther's promises "Taste as Big as Texas." Try it for yourself when you're in Houston and in a hurry or on a budget.

OTTO'S BAR-B-Q
5502 Memorial. (713) 864-2573
Cash / credit. Cafeteria style.

Otto's is best known as former president George Bush's favorite barbecue joint. And why not? With a selection of brisket, sausage links, chicken, ham, pork, turkey, and both beef and pork ribs, what's not to like? We found the brisket a little milder than most joints, but a dash of sauce took care of that.

TONY ROMA'S—A PLACE FOR RIBS
2232 FM 1960 W. (713) 893-7662
Cash / credit. Table service.
6356 Richmond Ave. (713) 952-7427
Cash / credit. Table service.
20033 I-45 (Gulf Fwy.). (713) 338-7427
Cash / credit. Table service.

This popular Dallas-based chain offers up a wide variety of ribs, served in an elegant atmosphere perfect for special occasions. (For a full description of the chain, see the Dallas section.)

LUBBOCK

The major metropolitan area of the vast South Plains, Lubbock has evolved from a small county seat to a modern center of technology, agriculture, medicine, and education. Early settlers of the area were a tough, self-reliant breed who faced drought, fire, and sandstorms to establish their place on the plains. Modern residents are proud of the many tourist attractions here, from an unparalleled Western ranching historic center to the Lubbock Walk of Fame to a barbecue pit that's known throughout the Lone Star State.

STUBB'S BAR-B-Q
620 19th St. (806) 747-4777
Cash. Table service / take out. Catering.

The Stubb's menu says "There will be no bad talk or loud talk at this place." Well, there's no reason to talk bad, but after a few bites of this tasty 'que, it's mighty hard to keep quiet—this is some of the best barbecue in west Texas.

Stubb's is the creation of Christopher "Stubb" Stubblefield, a Texas native who hails from the Lubbock area. Stubb traces his cooking roots back to his days as an Army mess sergeant during the Korean War.

Today Stubb's restaurant serves battalions of happy diners from around the state who've learned this is Mecca for both meat and music lovers. There's a natural marriage between barbecue and music, one Stubblefield has long recognized. His former Austin pit pulled in some of the best names in Texas music: Butch Hancock, Stevie Ray Vaughn, and Joe Ely, artists who've sang for their supper of brisket and ribs. When Stubblefield closed his Austin joint and moved the operation back to his hometown, he brought the blues with him. Diners can enjoy live music several nights a week.

But blues is only half the story. The rest is the smoky product of the pits: brisket, sausage, ribs (both pork and hefty beef ones), and chicken. We're happy to say that we've tried them all, served up with sides of beans, potato salad, rolls, and serrano peppers. The barbecue is accompanied by a delightfully peppery sauce that's available by mail (see Appendix B).

SOUTH PADRE ISLAND

When most travelers think of South Padre Island, the southernmost strip of island at the tip of Texas, they visualize spring break, winter Texans, and seafood. This stretch of commercial coastline is packed to the gills every March and April by partying spring-break revelers, then from November through February it's home to a quieter group of travelers, the winter Texans who come from the northern states and Canada to enjoy the most tropical of Texas climes. Busy Padre Boulevard is lined with condominiums, shops, and seafood restaurants, plus a prime South Texas smokehouse.

ROVANS BAKERY, RESTAURANT AND BBQ
5300 Padre Blvd. (210) 761-6972

Cash. Table service.

The sign says Rovans provides "home cooking for those who aren't home cooking." We can't think of a better way to describe this island cafe. This is one of the friendliest places we've visited, filled with locals and vacationers alike who come here in the morning to enjoy made-from-scratch pastries and a cup of coffee that never gets more than half empty. In the afternoon, diners return for mesquite-smoked barbecue, featuring brisket, chicken, baby back ribs, sausage, and chopped beef. We especially loved the ribs, kept in the smoker until the meat just about falls off the bone. The plates are served up with coleslaw, potato salad, pinto beans, and, a sign of the pit's proximity to Mexico, pico de gallo to spice up the meal.

While you're seated at Rovans, watch the miniature train that winds its way around the restaurant from tracks suspended from the ceiling.

PART THREE
AROUND THE PIT

Getting a barbecue recipe is a little like getting instructions on how to create art. Barbecuing is not an exact science, but rather something that relies on the creator's mood, his surroundings, or, as one cook-off competitor put it, "how much beer I've had to drink that day."

Nonetheless, we've put together this collection of recipes from the pits of Texas. Restaurateurs, volunteer firemen, barbecue teams, sauce makers, caterers, even the governor of Texas, have contributed their secrets. Regardless of their varied backgrounds, these folks have one thing in common: they're all barbecue artists, judging from their product.

RECIPE LISTING

BURNETT'S BARBECUE SAUCE

Tibb Burnett, a Texas poet and the author of Heart Spells, *passed along this sauce to us. The recipe, originating with Tibb's dad Glenn, is pure poetry. Tibb originally hails from the Benjamin area near the Panhandle and recalls when all the local barbecue joints used to serve stewed apricots as a side dish, a throwback to the days when chuck wagon cooks had to rely on dried provisions.*

4 cups tomato sauce

3/4 cup prepared mustard

1 tablespoon dried mustard

1 teaspoon black pepper

3/4 cup apple cider vinegar

1/4 cup Worcestershire sauce

1 tablespoon firmly packed brown sugar

1/2 cup water

6 cloves garlic, chopped

1 large onion, chopped

Juice and peel of 1/2 lemon

Combine tomato sauce, mustards, pepper, vinegar, Worcestershire, sugar, and water in a saucepan. Stir in garlic and onion, followed by lemon juice and peel. Simmer, covered, for at least 45 minutes. Cool and strain into jars.

MAKES ABOUT 3 PINTS

BAR-B-Q SAUCE VILLEGAS

If you travel to Fiesta Texas, San Antonio's theme park that showcases the many cultures of the Lone Star State, you'll have the chance to dine on barbecue by Oliver Villegas, 1991 Texas Chef of the Year. Even if you don't make it to the popular theme park, though, you can try your hand at his sauce.

2 cups minced onion

1/2 cup (1 stick) butter

2 cloves garlic, minced

2 cups chicken stock

1/2 cup white vinegar

1 teaspoon dry mustard

5 tablespoons Worcestershire sauce

2 tablespoons Chinese chili oil

2 tablespoons fresh lime juice

1 tablespoon Tabasco sauce

2 bay leaves

1/4 cup firmly packed brown sugar

In a heavy saucepan, sauté onion in butter until translucent. Add garlic and sauté for 2 minutes. Add remaining ingredients and simmer over low heat for 1 hour, stirring often.

MAKES 3 CUPS

GENE'S BARBECUE SAUCE

Gene Forsythe from Muldoon is a regular competitor at the Czhilispiel in Flatonia. When he's not making chili, he's making barbecue. "The most important thing after the meat is the sauce," swears Gene. The chef says the secret to this recipe is the dry mustard.

3 tablespoons dry mustard

1/2 cup (1 stick) plus
  2 tablespoons margarine
  or butter, melted

2 cups catsup

1/2 cup water

1/4 cup liquid smoke

1/2 cup Worcestershire or soy
  sauce

6 tablespoons firmly packed
  brown sugar

4 teaspoons celery seed

1 small onion, diced

In a saucepan, combine dry mustard and 1/2 cup melted butter. Stir in remaining ingredients except onion and begin simmering. In a sauté pan, sauté onion in remaining 2 tablespoons butter until translucent. Add onion to sauce and simmer for 30 minutes.

MAKES 2 TO 3 PINTS

GRANDDAD'S BARBECUE SAUCE

This easy-to-make barbecue sauce recipe was contributed by Linda Waggoner in the Travis County Extension Office. It originated with her husband's grandfather, who operated a barbecue stand for many years. Linda says, "Dab it on the meat with a swab or other brush if you have one, turn often, and keep dabbing on the other side and then back and forth. We never did measure much."

2 cups (4 sticks) butter (no substitute)

1/2 large bottle catsup

2 tablespoons prepared mustard

Dash or two of red hot sauce

1/2 large bottle of Worcestershire sauce

1/2 cup white vinegar

1 teaspoon chili powder

In a saucepan, melt butter and stir in remaining ingredients, varying quantities if desired to taste. Simmer for 15 minutes.

MAKES 2 TO 3 PINTS

GEORGETOWN VFD BAR-B-QUE SAUCE

The firemen of the Georgetown Volunteer Fire Department only like to see one kind of smoke: that from barbecue pits. Every fall, the firefighters cook a barbecue dinner to raise funds.

8 cups catsup

1/2 cup (1 stick) margarine

1/2 cup prepared mustard

1/2 cup soy sauce

Juice of 1 lemon

1/2 cup chopped onion

1/2 cup firmly packed brown sugar

6 drops Tabasco sauce

Salt and black pepper to taste

In a large saucepan, combine all ingredients, stirring to mix well. Simmer for 15 minutes.

MAKES ABOUT 2-1/2 QUARTS

CHARLENE HAHN'S SWEET 'N HOT BAR-BE-QUE SAUCE

Charlene and Duane Hahn, better known to cook-off competitors around Texas as the "Old Farts" team, contributed this recipe. This Temple couple says, "We live, sleep, and breathe barbecue. We make anywhere from 40 to 45 cook-offs a year." These active members of the Central Texas Barbecue Association admit that they've won and lost a lot of cook-offs, but they're having a great time. "We told our kids when we went to that BBQ cook-off in the sky to just go ahead and divide the trophies because we were spending the money now," confesses Charlene.

4 cups Heinz Chili sauce

2 cups maple-flavored pancake syrup

2 to 4 tablespoons honey or apply jelly to taste

Hot pepper sauce to taste

In a large bowl, combine all ingredients and stir well. Refrigerate unused portions.

MAKES ABOUT 6 CUPS

MICHAEL CONNER'S "BLACK MAGIC" BARBECUE SAUCE

Michael Conner is a chef at the Lake Austin Spa Resort, an elegant health resort located on the shores of Lake Austin. This recipe, like other dishes served there, is low fat and low calorie (only 11 calories and 1/4 gram of fat per teaspoon).

1/2 small onion, finely diced

1 tablespoon vegetable oil

1 clove garlic, minced

1/4 cup firmly packed brown sugar

2 tablespoons blackstrap molasses

1/2 cup Creole mustard

2 tablespoons Worcestershire sauce

1/4 cup dark beer

1-1/4 cups catsup

1 teaspoon Tabasco sauce

1/2 teaspoon cayenne pepper

1 tablespoon liquid smoke

1/2 cup apple cider vinegar

Sauté onion in vegetable oil over high heat until soft. Add garlic and brown sugar and reduce heat, stirring until sugar melts and darkens. Add all other ingredients and simmer over low heat, stirring occasionally, for 30 minutes. Serve as an accompaniment to smoked meats.

MAKES 1 QUART

SMOKE SIGNALS BARBECUE SAUCE

This sauce is the creation of El Paso Chile Company owners Park and Norma Kerr, authors of the Texas Border Cookbook. *The El Paso Chile Company itself is the creator of two tasty barbecue sauces (beer and tequila flavored), but if you want to try your hand at your own creation, here's a spicy way to get you started.*

3 tablespoons olive oil

1 cup minced onion

3 cloves garlic, minced

1 tablespoon mild chili powder blend

1 (28-ounce) can crushed tomatoes with liquid

1 (12-ounce) bottle amber beer (such as Dos Equis)

1 cup tomato-based bottled hot salsa

1/2 cup catsup

1/4 cup firmly packed light brown sugar

4 canned chipotles adobado, minced (reserve 3 tablespoons liquid)

2 tablespoons apple cider vinegar

2 tablespoons unsulfured molasses

1/2 teaspoon liquid smoke

1/2 teaspoon salt

In a heavy 3-quart saucepan over low heat, warm olive oil. Add onion and garlic, cover, and cook, stirring once or twice, for 10 minutes. Stir in chili powder blend and cook, covered, for 5 minutes more.

Stir in crushed tomatoes, beer, salsa, catsup, brown sugar, chipotles plus reserved liquid, vinegar, molasses, liquid smoke, and salt, and bring to a simmer. Cook, partially covered, stirring once or twice, until sauce has thickened slightly and is shiny (about 30 minutes).

Cool sauce to room temperature and, if you prefer a smooth texture, force it through the medium blade of a food mill or puree in a food processor. Transfer to a storage container and refrigerate. (*Note:* Sauce can be refrigerated for several weeks or frozen up to 3 months.)

MAKES ABOUT 2 QUARTS

TROPICAL BARBECUE SAUCE

This Lake Austin Spa Resort creation has a mere 28 calories and only a trace of fat per tablespoon. It will add an island zing to your barbecue with its sweet and sour flavors.

1 cup molasses
1/2 cup apple cider vinegar
1/4 cup Worcestershire sauce
2 tablespoons Dijon mustard
1 teaspoon PickaPeppa sauce
1/4 cup fresh orange juice

Combine all ingredients and whirl in a food processor. Use to baste or sauce grilled chicken or pork tenderloin.

MAKES ABOUT 2 CUPS

CRANBERRY BARBECUE SAUCE

Why not barbecue a holiday turkey? With this recipe from the National Turkey Federation, you can add a seasonal taste to the bird.

1 (8-ounce) can jellied cranberry sauce

1/4 cup firmly packed brown sugar

1/4 cup prepared mustard

2 tablespoons fresh lemon juice

1 teaspoon Worcestershire sauce

1/8 teaspoon garlic powder

In a glass bowl, combine all ingredients and mix well. During the last hour of cooking, baste turkey with glaze every 15 minutes.

MAKES ABOUT 1-1/2 CUPS

TANGY TURKEY BARBECUE SAUCE

Give your turkey a sweet-and-sour tanginess with this recipe contributed by the National Turkey Federation.

1/2 cup pineapple juice

1/2 cup catsup

2 tablespoons white wine vinegar

2 tablespoons honey

2 teaspoons Kitchen Bouquet

1-1/2 teaspoons prepared mustard

Dash of hot pepper sauce

In a glass bowl, combine all ingredients and mix well. During the last hour of cooking, baste turkey with sauce every 15 minutes.

MAKES ABOUT 1-1/4 CUPS

SOUTHWESTERN GRILL

San Antonio viewers of KENS-TV are familiar with Patsy Swendson and her popular noontime cooking segments. Patsy is also the author of nearly a dozen cookbooks, ranging from breakfast recipes to sauces to cuisine for canines and felines. This recipe comes from her book Simply San Antonio, *available from Cookbooks by Patsy Swendson, P.O. Box TV5, San Antonio, TX 78299.*

3/4 cup packed fresh cilantro

2 jalapeño peppers, minced

1 tablespoon fresh lime juice

1 teaspoon grated lime zest

1/2 cup (1 stick) butter, softened

Salt to taste

Cayenne pepper to taste

Combine cilantro, jalapeños, and lime juice and zest in a food processor, and finely chop. Whirl in butter, salt, and cayenne pepper to blend. Transfer mixture to a saucepan and heat gently. Use as a baste when grilling chicken, fish, seafood, or vegetables.

BRISKET RUB

This recipe comes from Fritz's Capitol City Catering of Austin. When these people cook, they really cook. The following recipe makes enough rub for 21 briskets. Don't despair, though; the leftover rub stores well.

1 cup sugar

1 cup salt

1/2 cup chili powder

1/4 cup garlic powder

1/2 cup black pepper

Combine all ingredients and store in a tightly covered container. Rub 2-1/2 tablespoons of mixture onto brisket prior to cooking.

MAKES 3-1/2 CUPS

SOUTHWESTERN RUB

Spice up your meats with this recipe from the Texas Beef Industry Council. It yields enough to season 2 pounds of beef.

1-1/2 teaspoons chili powder

1 teaspoon garlic powder

1/2 teaspoon dried oregano leaves, crushed

1/4 teaspoon ground cumin

Combine all ingredients in a small bowl and stir well. Use to season tender beef steaks such as sirloin, T-bone, Porterhouse, tenderloin, rib eye, and top loin.

MAKES ABOUT 1 TABLESPOON

BEST OF THE BORDER DRY RUB

This recipe appears courtesy of Bob Matzig and Bill Langford, members of the Del Rio Chamber of Commerce Chuck Wagon Gang. They put it to work on their Best of the Border Barbecue Brisket (see recipe on p. 93).

12 tablespoons salt

8 tablespoons black pepper

2 tablespoons chili powder

3 tablespoons garlic powder

3 tablespoons cayenne pepper

8 tablespoons MSG (optional)

Combine all ingredients and store in an airtight container. Use as a rub for brisket.

MAKES ABOUT 2-1/4 CUPS

BARBECUE MARINADE

Spend 10 minutes in the kitchen preparing this easy marinade from the Texas Beef Industry Council and use it to marinate 1 to 1-1/2 pounds of beef. Reserve and refrigerate a portion of unused marinade for basting during cooking. Always marinate meat in the refrigerator, in a heavy-duty plastic bag or glass utility dish. Discard any leftover marinade that has been in contact with raw meat.

1/2 cup chopped onion

1-1/2 tablespoons firmly packed brown sugar

1 tablespoon vegetable oil

1/3 cup apple cider vinegar

1/3 cup catsup

1 tablespoon prepared horseradish

1 tablespoon water

1/4 teaspoon coarse black pepper

In a small saucepan over medium heat, sauté onion and brown sugar in oil until onion is tender (about 3 minutes). Add remaining ingredients and simmer over medium heat for 3 or 4 minutes, stirring occasionally. Remove from heat and cool thoroughly before adding to beef.

MAKES ABOUT 3/4 CUP

MEXICALI MARINADE

Give up to 2 pounds of meat a Tex-Mex flair with this recipe from the Texas Beef Industry Council. The Council advises that most beef must marinate for at least 6 hours for tenderizing to take place (shorter periods will suffice to infuse flavor into tender cuts). Marinating longer than 24 hours causes surface meat fibers to break down and produce a mushy texture.

1/2 cup prepared salsa (mild, medium, or hot, as desired)

2 tablespoons chopped cilantro or parsley

2 tablespoons fresh lime juice

1 tablespoon vegetable oil

Combine all ingredients, stirring until well blended. Use to tenderize and flavor beef steaks such as eye of the round, top round, flank, and chuck, or just to season tender beef steaks such as sirloin, T-bone, Porterhouse, tenderloin, rib eye, and top loin.

MAKES ABOUT 2/3 CUP

TERIYAKI BEEF BRISKET MARINADE

This sweet-and-sour marinade was contributed by Charlene Hahn, a well-known barbecue competitor in the Lone Star State. Use it to marinade a 6- to 8-pound brisket overnight.

1 cup pineapple juice

1 cup soy sauce

1/2 cup firmly packed dark brown sugar

1/2 teaspoon ground ginger

1/2 teaspoon garlic powder

1 teaspoon gin or rum

2 teaspoons cornstarch

1/2 cup cold water

In a saucepan, combine pineapple juice, soy sauce, brown sugar, ginger, garlic, and liquor. Stir well and bring to boil. In a bowl, blend cornstarch and water, and then stir into boiling sauce. Simmer for 2 minutes, then remove from heat. Let mixture cool to room temperature before using on meat.

MAKES ABOUT 3 CUPS

BEST OF THE BORDER BARBECUE BRISKET

This recipe was created by Bob Matzig and Bill Langford of the Del Rio Chamber of Commerce Chuck Wagon Gang. These guys prepare barbecue for various chamber events throughout the year. Del Rio is an oasis at the edge of the Chihuahua desert, a place best known for beautiful Lake Amistad on the U.S.-Mexico border and for the ancient Indian pictographs at Seminole Canyon.

9- to 10-pound brisket

5 tablespoons Best of the Border Dry Rub (see recipe on p. 89)

1/4 cup full-flavor beer

Barbecue sauce (your choice)

Preheat barbecue pit to 250 degrees. Cut off fat wedge near large end of brisket, then pat dry rub evenly over meat. Place brisket in barbecue pit, fat-side up, and cook at 250 to 275 degrees for 4 hours.

Remove meat from pit. Make a foil bag large enough to hold brisket from extra-heavy-duty foil, leaving one side open. Put meat in bag and add beer. Seal all edges of foil well.

Return brisket in bag to the pit. Raise temperature to 300 degrees. Let pit cook back down to 225 to 250 degrees and cook another 3 hours. Remove brisket from pit, top with favorite barbecue sauce, slice, and serve.

SERVES 16 TO 20

MARINATED SMOKED BRISKET WITH CHIPOTLE PEPPER AU JUS

When you're ready for something a little fancier than the traditional brisket, whip out this recipe by Renie Steves from the Texas Beef Industry Council.

5-pound brisket

3/4 cup red raspberry vinegar

1/4 cup balsamic vinegar

1/4 cup Worcestershire sauce

1/4 cup peanut oil

1/4 cup soy sauce

1 teaspoon mustard oil (Oriental)

1 teaspoon mustard seed

3 dried hot red chile peppers

4 cloves garlic, coarsely chopped

1/2 medium onion, coarsely chopped

1/2 cup mango chutney

1 tablespoon maple syrup

1 tablespoon fresh lemon juice

1 teaspoon salt

1/4 teaspoon black pepper

3 chipotle peppers

1-1/4 cups brown stock

1 tablespoon arrowroot

Trim brisket of most fat. Place all ingredients except brisket, chipotle peppers, brown stock, and arrowroot in a resealable plastic bag and mix well. Add brisket, making sure it is well immersed in the marinade. Marinate for 24 to 48 hours, turning the bag occasionally.

Prepare smoker. After 45 to 60 minutes, add apple wood or other flavored wood that has been soaked in water for at least 30 minutes. Remove meat from bag and reserve marinade. Smoke meat for 2 to 2-1/2 hours, or until internal temperature reaches 125 degrees for rare or 140 to 145 degrees for medium. Remove meat and wrap in foil to keep warm. When serving, slice across the grain.

To make sauce, pour reserved marinade (about 2-1/2 to 3 cups) into a small saucepan and add chipotle peppers. Simmer for about 30 minutes, then remove from heat and let cool to room temperature. Strain and degrease.

Pour cooked marinade (about 1-1/2 cups) back into a saucepan. Add 1 cup brown stock and stir. Dissolve arrowroot in remaining 1/4 cup brown stock and stir mixture into sauce. Allow to remain over heat until hot. Adjust seasoning if necessary and serve over smoked brisket.

SERVES 8 TO 10

EASY BRISKET

Dr. Bob Morgan likes this easy-to-make recipe for a no-fail brisket.

5-pound brisket
Small jar of prepared mustard
Barbecue sauce (your choice)

Coat brisket with prepared mustard. Smoke meat overnight, for at least 16 hours. Remove brisket from smoker and wrap in foil. Place in a 225-degree oven for 3 hours. Slice and serve with your favorite barbecue sauce.

SERVES 8 TO 10

GENE'S BARBECUED BEEF

The former owner of the general store in Muldoon once sold his meats in the little store near La Grange. Today Gene Forsythe cooks for family get-togethers and local reunions, serving up this delicious brisket.

4- to 6-pound brisket, 2-1/2 inches thick

1 cup catsup

1/2 cup water

1/3 cup white vinegar

1/4 cup vegetable oil

1 tablespoon instant coffee

1 teaspoon salt

1/2 teaspoon black pepper

1 teaspoon chili powder

1 teaspoon celery seed

1/8 teaspoon garlic powder

1 teaspoon hot sauce

Using a sharp knife, score the fat edges of brisket. In a bowl, combine remaining ingredients. Reserve and refrigerate 1/2 cup of marinade mixture. Place brisket in a shallow glass baking dish and top with remaining marinade. Cover and refrigerate overnight, turning brisket several times.

Remove brisket from marinade and pat dry. Discard used marinade. Cook meat over hot coals for 4 to 6 hours. During the last 15 to 20 minutes, baste meat with reserved marinade.

SERVES 8 TO 12

GENE'S SIMPLE BARBECUE BRISKET

When you don't have time for the long version, here's a simple brisket from Gene Forsythe.

3- to 4-pound brisket

Meat tenderizer

1 teaspoon chili powder

1 teaspoon brisket rub (your choice)

2 cups Italian salad dressing

Sprinkle meat with tenderizer. Brush brisket with combined chili powder, rub, and salad dressing. Cook in a smoker for 3 to 4 hours, then slice and serve.

SERVES 6 TO 8

BRISKET SALAD

This recipe comes from Claude's Sauces in El Paso, a company that has been making brisket sauces for over 20 years.

1/2 pound shredded cooked brisket, cooked in Claude's Brisket Sauce

1/2 medium-sized head lettuce, cut into bite-sized pieces

1 large tomato, cut into small pieces

1 small purple onion, sliced into rings

1/2 cup chopped green pepper

1/2 cup chopped red pepper

1 small cucumber, coarsely chopped

1/2 cup black olives

1/2 cup grated hard cheese (such as Parmesan)

Italian salad dressing to taste

Dash of dried crushed oregano

Combine meat with lettuce, tomato, onion, peppers, cucumber, olives, and cheese. Add salad dressing and oregano, and toss gently. Refrigerate until ready to serve.

SERVES 4

BARBECUED FLANK STEAK

This favorite recipe comes from Karen Haram, food editor of the San Antonio Express-News *and author of* San Antonio Cuisine, *a collection of Alamo City recipes set for publication in summer 1994 by Two Lane Press.*

1-1/2-pound flank steak

3 cloves garlic, minced

1/2 cup vegetable oil

1/2 cup tomato juice

1/2 cup soy sauce

1/2 cup firmly packed brown sugar

1/2 teaspoon black pepper

Using a sharp knife, score flank steak on each side in a diamond pattern about 1/8-inch deep. Place in a glass baking dish and set aside. Combine remaining ingredients and pour over steak. Refrigerate, covered, for 24 hours, turning meat several times. Let stand at room temperature for 2 hours before grilling.

Preheat grill. Pour off marinade from meat and transfer liquid to a small saucepan. Heat to the boiling point, then strain into another saucepan and keep warm.

Grill meat over high heat for 4 to 5 minutes per side. Thinly slice steak across the grain immediately (flank steak can get tough upon standing) and serve topped with warm sauce.

SERVES 2 TO 4

BARBECUED SHORT RIBS

This recipe, contributed by Pace Foods of San Antonio, combines two Texas favorites: barbecued beef ribs and picante sauce, a condiment that's as popular as catsup in the Lone Star State.

6 pounds meaty beef short ribs, trimmed of visible fat

1 teaspoon salt

2 medium onions, finely chopped

2 cloves garlic, minced

1/4 cup vegetable oil

2 cups catsup

1-1/2 cups Pace Picante Sauce

4 teaspoons fresh lemon juice

1/4 cup firmly packed brown sugar

2 teaspoons ground cumin

In a large heavy skillet or Dutch oven, brown meat in its own fat over medium-low heat, then drain thoroughly. Sprinkle meat in pan with salt. Cover tightly and cook over low heat, turning frequently, for 1-1/2 to 2 hours or until tender. (At this point, meat may be removed from skillet, covered, and refrigerated for up to 24 hours.)

In a small saucepan, sauté onions and garlic in oil until onions are tender but not brown. Add remaining ingredients (except meat) and bring to a boil. Reduce heat and simmer uncovered for 8 to 10 minutes, stirring frequently.

Arrange meat on the grill over hot coals, 5 to 6 inches from heat. Brush generously with some of the sauce mixture. Barbecue for 20 to 30 minutes or until meat is well glazed, frequently turning and basting with sauce. Heat remaining sauce and serve with meat.

SERVES 6

ROUGE RIBS

Austin's King's Rouge Sauce sends this easy-to-follow recipe for sure-fire ribs. You can substitute pork ribs for the beef if you choose.

6 pounds beef ribs

1 teaspoon salt

1 tablespoon black pepper

1 teaspoon garlic powder

1 (16-ounce) jar King's Rouge Sauce

Rub salt, pepper, and garlic powder onto ribs. Place meat on the grill and cook for about 25 minutes until approximately three-quarters done. Spoon or brush on King's Rouge Sauce and continue cooking for another 8 to 10 minutes until done.

SERVES 6

TEXAS-STYLE PORK BARBECUE

This recipe from the National Pork Producers is the perfect solution to leftover pork.

3/4 pound boneless cooked pork loin, thinly sliced

1/4 cup coarsely chopped onion

1 clove garlic, minced

2 teaspoons butter

3/4 cup chili sauce

1 tablespoon firmly packed brown sugar

1 tablespoon white vinegar

1 tablespoon molasses

1 tablespoon water

1 teaspoon fresh lemon juice

1 teaspoon prepared mustard

1/4 teaspoon liquid smoke

1/8 teaspoon cayenne pepper

1/8 teaspoon salt

4 onion rolls, split and toasted

In a medium saucepan, sauté onion and garlic in butter until tender. Stir in chili sauce, sugar, vinegar, molasses, water, lemon juice, mustard, liquid smoke, cayenne pepper, and salt. Bring to a boil, then reduce heat and simmer, uncovered, for about 15 minutes. Add pork slices to mixture, stirring gently to coat meat with sauce. Continue simmering for about 5 minutes, until pork is heated through. Serve on toasted onion rolls with extra sauce on the side.

SERVES 4

TEXAS-STYLE BARBECUED PORK CHOPS

When you're short on time or good weather, bring the barbecue inside with this recipe from the National Pork Producers Council.

6 center loin pork chops, 1-inch thick

1/2 cup finely chopped onion

1/2 cup finely chopped celery

1 tablespoon vegetable oil

1 cup catsup

1/2 cup molasses

1/2 cup water

2 tablespoons red wine vinegar

2 teaspoons dry mustard

1/4 teaspoon cayenne pepper, or to taste

1/4 teaspoon salt

Heat vegetable oil in a medium saucepan and sauté onion and celery over medium-low heat for 5 minutes. Stir in remaining ingredients and mix well. Bring to a boil, then reduce heat and simmer for 15 minutes, stirring occasionally.

Place pork chops on a broiler pan 5 inches from heat. Broil for about 8 minutes on each side, brushing frequently with sauce. Serve with remaining sauce, if desired.

SERVES 4 TO 6

PEACHY SMOKED PORK ROAST

The National Pork Producers Council offers this recipe for pork roast filled with smoky flavor and the sweetness of one of central Texas's favorite crops: peaches.

2-pound boneless pork loin roast

1 tablespoon salt

1/2 teaspoon black pepper

1 teaspoon ground ginger

2 tablespoons vegetable oil

2 tablespoons apple cider vinegar

1/2 cup firmly packed brown sugar

3 tablespoons bottled chili sauce

1 (29-ounce) can peach slices in heavy syrup, undrained

In a blender or food processor, combine salt, pepper, ginger, oil, vinegar, brown sugar, chili sauce, and undrained peaches. Whirl until smooth. Place pork loin in a heavy resealable plastic bag and add half of peach sauce. Refrigerate, covered, overnight. Refrigerate remaining peach sauce.

Prepare grill, surrounding drip pan with medium-hot coals (if using a gas grill, heat to medium temperature). Add hickory chips, soaked with water, to heat source. Place pork on grill over drip pan. Baste often with marinade until internal temperature reaches 155 to 160 degrees (about 60 minutes). Let stand for 10 minutes, then slice thinly and serve with reserved peach sauce, heated.

SERVES 8

R-D PORK BARBECUE

When you're in the mood to stray from traditional Texas barbecue, try this recipe from the National Pork Producers that makes a tart rather than toma-toey product.

4-pound boneless pork shoulder (Boston butt)

1 quart apple cider vinegar

1 tablespoon crushed dried red pepper

1 tablespoon black pepper

Stir together vinegar and peppers. Prepare medium-hot coals in a covered grill, banking coals when hot. Position drip pan in center of bed, between banks of coals. Place pork on grill over drip pan and close hood. Cook for 2-1/2 to 3-1/2 hours, basting frequently with vinegar-pepper mixture, until meat is very tender. Remove pork from cooker and cool slightly, then chop and serve.

SERVES 12 TO 16

STEVE WELCH'S BABY BACK RIBS

This recipe is not short on ingredients, but it's long on flavor.

12 to 14 pounds baby back pork ribs

2-1/2 cups finely diced onions

10 (8-ounce) cans tomato sauce

7-1/2 cups water

2 cups minus 1 tablespoon apple cider vinegar

1-1/4 cups Worcestershire sauce

2-1/2 cups firmly packed brown sugar

1-1/4 cups soy sauce

1 to 3 tablespoons salt to taste (optional)

1 teaspoon paprika

3 tablespoons plus 1 teaspoon chili powder

2 tablespoons black pepper

2-1/2 teaspoons ground cinnamon

1-1/2 teaspoons ground cloves

1/2 cup (1 stick) butter

1-1/2 teaspoons cayenne pepper

In a saucepan, combine all ingredients except ribs. Bring to a boil and simmer for 10 minutes. Let cool to room temperature.

Remove thin membrane from bone side of ribs. Cut meat to almost separate individual ribs and place in a large resealable plastic bag. Add cooked sauce, reserving some to use later as a baste. Marinate, refrigerated, for 24 hours.

Remove meat from marinade, bring to room temperature, and place on a prepared grill. Barbecue over hot coals (Steve recommends using mesquite), basting constantly until done. Cook until blackened.

SERVES 15

COWBOY BARBECUED RIBS

The National Pork Producers contributed this easy-to-prepare rib recipe.

5 pounds pork spareribs
1 cup water
1/3 cup butter or margarine
2 tablespoons fresh lemon juice
1/4 cup dry mustard
1/4 cup chili powder
1 tablespoon sugar
1 tablespoon paprika
2 teaspoons salt
1 teaspoon onion powder
1 teaspoon garlic powder
1/4 teaspoon cayenne pepper

Place spareribs on a broiler pan, cover with foil, and roast at 400 degrees for 1-1/2 hours.

Meanwhile, combine remaining ingredients in a medium saucepan and stir well. Bring to a boil, then reduce heat and simmer for 30 minutes. Remove from heat.

Brush sauce on ribs and return to oven, broiling 5 inches from heat for 7 to 10 minutes per side. Serve ribs with additional sauce.

SERVES 6

ORANGE COUNTRY-STYLE RIBS

The National Pork Producers offered us this sweet recipe.

2 pounds country-style pork
   ribs

1 (6-ounce) can tomato paste

1/2 cup firmly packed brown
   sugar

1/4 cup thawed frozen orange
   juice concentrate

2 tablespoons red wine vinegar

1 tablespoon prepared mustard

1 tablespoon Worcestershire
   sauce

1/2 teaspoon black pepper

Cut meat into single-rib portions. Combine remaining ingredients, mix well, and set aside.

Place a large piece of foil over coals beneath the grill to catch drippings. Place ribs on grill, about 6 inches above slow coals. Close hood and cook for about 20 minutes. Turn ribs and cook, covered, for 20 minutes more. Brush ribs with sauce mixture and cook, covered, for 25 to 35 minutes more or until done, turning and basting frequently with sauce. Serve hot.

SERVES 4

PEACH-GLAZED PORK RIBS

When you can't barbecue outdoors, cook up some mighty tasty pork ribs indoors with this recipe. It comes from Peaches 'n Cream, *a book by the owner of Tru-Tex Products, producers of barbecue sauces and marinades. (See Appendix B for additional information.)*

4 to 4-1/2 pounds pork ribs, cut into serving pieces

1 to 1-1/2 cups picante sauce

1-1/2 cups peach preserves

1/4 cup soy sauce

Place ribs in a shallow roasting pan, meaty-side up. Roast uncovered in a 350-degree oven for 45 minutes.

In a saucepan, combine picante sauce, preserves, and soy sauce, and heat to boiling, stirring constantly. Remove from heat and set aside.

Brush pork with about 1/2 cup of sauce mixture and return to oven for 45 to 60 minutes more, until tender. Baste ribs several times while roasting.

SERVES 5 TO 6

KING'S WINGS

Make easy appetizers with this recipe from King's Rouge Sauce.

12 chicken wings

2 tablespoons Cajun seasoning

1 (16-ounce) jar King's Rouge Sauce

Place chicken wings and sauce in a large resealable plastic bag and marinate, refrigerated, for at least 2 hours.

Remove chicken wings from marinade and sprinkle with Cajun seasoning. Cook in a smoker or off the fire on a covered grill until done, about 20 minutes.

SERVES 4 TO 6

NO-TOMATO BARBECUED CHICKEN

Texas barbecue sauce is traditionally tomato based, but when you're ready for a break, try this one sent to us by the Texas Poultry Federation.

8 pieces broiler-fryer chicken parts

3-1/2 tablespoons butter

1 tablespoon minced onion

1/4 cup fresh lemon juice

1-1/2 teaspoons prepared mustard

1 teaspoon salt

1 teaspoon firmly packed brown sugar

1 teaspoon Worcestershire sauce

1/4 teaspoon black pepper

3 to 4 drops hot pepper sauce

1/3 cup water

In a small saucepan, melt butter over medium-high heat. Add onion and sauté until onion is translucent, about 5 minutes. Add lemon juice, mustard, salt, brown sugar, Worcestershire sauce, pepper, and hot pepper sauce, stirring well. Slowly add water, then stir until mixture boils. Remove from heat.

Brush chicken pieces with sauce and place on a prepared grill, skin-side up, about 8 inches from heat. Cook, turning and basting with sauce every 10 to 15 minutes, for about 1 hour or until a fork can be inserted into meat with ease.

SERVES 4 TO 6

TEXAS BEER CHICKEN

Texas beer chicken is an easy-to-make recipe contributed by the "Living on the Edge" barbecue team from Houston. Led by head cook Allen Shepherd, the team specializes in two things: brisket and benefits. "We do a lot of benefits around Houston for kids, like the Make-A-Wish Foundation and the D.A.R.E. program," Shepherd explains. "Our main objective is to help children who need help." The group performs an adult comedy routine in the evenings at cook-offs, after they've spent the day tending the fires. These guys have been cooking for seven years, and they turn out some of the tenderest product found at area cook-offs. This unorthodox recipe for Texas beer chicken is one of the easiest, moistest chicken recipes you'll ever run across.

3- to 5-pound whole chicken

1 (12-ounce) can of beer

Seasonings to taste

Rinse chicken, pat dry, and season as you choose. Open can of beer and slide bird over it, so that can inserts into cavity of chicken. Stand the can (and the upright bird) in the cooker for 5-1/2 hours at 160 degrees.

SERVES 4 TO 6

SMOKED TURKEY

The National Turkey Federation recommends the following method for smoking a turkey. To try a couple of their turkey barbecue sauces, see the recipes on pages 84 and 85.

10- to 14-pound turkey

Before cooking, remove neck and giblets from body cavity. Skewer neck skin to back of bird, tuck wings akimbo behind the back, and place legs in a hock lock or tie them loosely together with string.

To smoke turkey, add a few water-soaked hickory or fruitwood chips to charcoal every half hour. Meat thermometer should register 160 degrees when done.

SERVES 8 TO 10

WHITE WINGS

Serve this smoked dove as an appetizer or a main dish. The chef at the South-fork Ranch, J.R.'s TV home, provided the tasty recipe.

3 pounds dove meat (chicken breast may be substituted)

3 to 4 tablespoons seasoned salt

2 tablespoons Cajun seasoning

1/2 pound sharp cheddar cheese, cut into 1/2-inch cubes

10 jalapeño peppers, halved and seeds removed, cut into 1/2-inch pieces

1 pound bacon, cut into 5-inch strips

Poach meat in gently boiling water along with seasoned salt and Cajun seasoning for 15 minutes or until tender. Drain and let cool for 30 minutes.

Pull or cut meat into 1-by-3-by-1/4-inch strips. Wrap a strip of meat around a cube of cheese and piece of pepper, then wrap a strip of bacon around the meat bundle and secure with a toothpick. Repeat process with remaining ingredients. Put bundles in a smoker and cook until bacon is done and cheese has melted.

MAKES 20 HORS D'OEUVRES

BARBECUED CATFISH

This recipe was contributed by Linda Waggoner, a Travis County Extension Office home economist.

6 small catfish, skinned

1 teaspoon Worcestershire sauce

1/8 teaspoon paprika

1/2 cup vegetable oil

1/4 cup white vinegar

1/4 cup catsup

2 tablespoons sugar

1/4 teaspoon salt

1/4 teaspoon black pepper

Clean and fillet catfish. Combine remaining ingredients and brush some of mixture onto fillets. Place fish on a well-greased grill, 3 to 4 inches from hot coals, for about 5 minutes per side or until fillets test done. Brush frequently with remaining sauce during grilling.

SERVES 6

EASY BARBECUED CATFISH STEAKS

This is an even easier version of barbecued catfish, also provided by Linda Waggoner.

**3 pounds catfish steaks,
  3/4-inch thick**

Juice of 1 lemon

1/4 cup vegetable oil

**1/4 cup barbecue sauce (your
  choice)**

Place catfish steaks in a shallow glass baking dish. Combine lemon juice and oil and pour over steaks. Cover and refrigerate for 30 minutes, turning once.

Place barbecue sauce in a saucepan and bring to simmering point. Remove catfish from marinade and arrange in a folding wire grilling basket. Brush well with warm barbecue sauce. Cook 3 to 4 inches from hot coals for about 3 minutes or until golden brown. Brush with additional sauce, then turn and cook for 2 to 3 minutes more. Brush with sauce and serve.

SERVES 4 TO 6

BILLY BLUES SHRIMP BOLTS

This recipe offers a chance to combine some of Texas's best ingredients: shrimp, barbecue, and grapefruit. Using Billy Blues Hot Lightnin' Bolt Barbecue Sauce will make your shrimp extra spicy; substitute a milder sauce if you need to tone it down.

1 pound medium to large shrimp, shelled and deveined

3/4 cup Billy Blues Hot Lightnin' Bolt Barbecue Sauce

1/3 cup fresh grapefruit juice

1 teaspoon grated fresh ginger

2 cloves garlic, minced

Combine barbecue sauce, grapefruit juice, ginger, and garlic in a large glass bowl. Pour off 1/4 cup of mixture and set aside for later use. Add shrimp to remaining mixture and marinate in the refrigerator for at least 1 to 2 hours.

Remove shrimp from marinade and barbecue over hot coals for 2 minutes per side, basting frequently with reserved marinade. (*Note:* These are delicious with a dipping sauce made of 3 tablespoons melted butter and 1/4 cup Billy Blues Hot Lightnin' Bolt Barbecue Sauce.)

SERVES 4

LEMON BARBECUED SHRIMP

This recipe using fresh Gulf shrimp was contributed by Travis County Extension Office home economist Linda Waggoner.

2-1/2 pounds unpeeled large shrimp

1/2 cup fresh lemon juice

1/4 cup reduced-calorie Italian salad dressing

1/4 cup water

1/4 cup soy sauce

3 tablespoons minced fresh parsley

3 tablespoons minced onion

1 clove garlic, crushed

1/2 teaspoon black pepper

Peel and devein shrimp, then place in a large shallow glass baking dish. Combine remaining ingredients in a jar, cover tightly, and shake vigorously. Pour 3/4 of the mixture over shrimp, reserving remainder for later use. Cover shrimp and refrigerate for 4 hours.

Remove shrimp from marinade and thread onto skewers. Grill 5 to 6 inches from heat for 3 to 4 minutes per side, basting frequently with reserved marinade.

SERVES 6

BACON ROUGE SHRIMP

Serve this dish from Austin's King's Rouge Sauce as an appetizer or main course.

25 medium to large shrimp, peeled and deveined

1/4 pound bacon, cut into 1-inch pieces

1 tablespoon fresh lemon juice

1 (16-ounce) jar King's Rouge Sauce

Wrap bacon pieces around shrimp and secure with toothpicks. Arrange in shallow glass baking dishes. Add lemon juice to King's Rouge Sauce, stir, and set aside 1/4 cup for later use. Pour remaining mixture over bacon-wrapped shrimp. Cover and marinate in refrigerator for at least 2 hours.

Remove shrimp bundles from marinade and place on prepared grill. Baste with reserved sauce while grilling. Cook until bacon is fully done. (*Note:* Watch for flareups caused by bacon drippings!)

SERVES 4 TO 6

GOVERNOR ANN RICHARDS'S SOUTHWESTERN PILAF

Every good barbecue needs some good side dishes, and this is one of the governor's favorites.

11-3/4 cups water

1 cup Texmati white rice, uncooked

1 cup Texmati brown rice, uncooked

1 cup wheat berries

1-1/2 cups dry black beans

1/4 pound salt pork

1 onion peeled and left whole, plus 1-1/2 cups finely diced onion

2 cloves garlic, peeled and left whole

2 tablespoons olive oil

1-1/2 cups finely diced celery

2 teaspoons garlic powder

2 teaspoons white pepper

2 teaspoons ground cumin

Salt to taste

In a saucepan, combine white and brown rice with 3-3/4 cups of water and simmer, covered, until rice is done (about 25 minutes). (Don't overcook and don't add salt.) Rinse rice in cold water and drain well. Set aside.

In another saucepan, combine wheat berries with 4 cups of water and simmer until done (about 90 minutes). Rinse in cold water and drain well. Set aside.

Rinse black beans thoroughly, then transfer to a saucepan and simmer in 4 cups of water seasoned with salt pork, whole onion, and garlic cloves. When done (after about 90 minutes), remove salt pork, onion, and garlic cloves, and discard. Rinse beans in cold water and drain well. Set aside.

Heat olive oil in a skillet and sauté combined celery, diced onion, garlic powder, pepper, and cumin until vegetables are translucent (about 5 minutes). In a large bowl, fold all ingredients together and add salt to taste. Transfer to a baking dish, cover with foil, and heat in a 350-degree oven for 20 to 25 minutes.

SERVES 12 TO 14

DIXIELAND DELIGHT'S PINTO BEANS

The members of Thorndale's Dixieland Delight barbecue team say there's one secret to making good beans: "Put 'em on and let 'em go." These fellows don't worry too much about their beans, and they sure don't worry about the recipe. They say that the beans turn out a little different every time, depending on what spices they have at hand. After lots of discussion, however, they've come up with a recipe for their super spicy beans. Do like the Dixieland Delight guys do—throw in a shake of this and a sprinkle of that, sit it all on the firebox, and just let 'em go.

1 pound dry pinto beans

2 cans Rotel diced tomatoes and chiles

3 shakes of salt

Sprinkle of ground cumin

1/2 teaspoon hot chili powder

Pinch of paprika

Pinch of cayenne pepper

Sprinkle of dried basil

2 shakes of black pepper

3 jalapeño peppers, sliced

1/2 pound bacon

1 1015 onion, diced

Rinse beans and soak covered in water overnight. Drain beans, rinse well, and transfer to a large pot. Add remaining ingredients and cover with fresh water. Cover pot and cook on a firebox for about 6 hours or on the stove for 5 to 6 hours. (If cooking on the stove, check more frequently and stir to keep beans from sticking and burning.)

SERVES 12

COUNTY LINE'S BEANS

The County Line, the immensely popular chain of upscale barbecue restaurants that began in Austin, has two recipes for tasty beans. When the cupboard is half empty, there's the simple version with just nine ingredients. When you're fully stocked, pull out all the stops for the version with pork and molasses.

CHUCK WAGON–STYLE BEANS

1 pound dry pinto beans

1/2 cup diced onions

1 tablespoon salt, or to taste

1 teaspoon black pepper, or to taste

1 tablespoon firmly packed brown sugar

2 tablespoons chili powder

1/2 teaspoon garlic powder

1/4 teaspoon celery salt

1/2 cup chopped bacon

Rinse beans thoroughly. Place all ingredients in a large stockpot. Add enough water to cover beans with 3 inches of water. Bring to a boil, then reduce flame and simmer over medium heat, stirring occasionally and adding water when needed. Cook until beans are tender.

SERVES 6 TO 8

TEXAS BARBECUED BEANS

2 pounds dry pinto beans

1 tablespoon salt

1 whole onion, peeled and split through (secure with 2 wooden picks to hold together)

2 large cloves garlic, with a wooden pick inserted into each

1/4 pound salt pork, slab bacon, or smoked jaw

1/3 cup shortening

2 cups very finely minced onions

1/2 cup all-purpose flour

2 cups tomato juice (or 3/4 cup tomato sauce, or 1/3 cup tomato paste diluted to make 2 cups)

Salt and black pepper to taste

1/4 cup firmly packed brown sugar

1/4 cup molasses

Tabasco sauce to taste

Soak beans overnight in water to cover plus 2 quarts. Discard water and rinse beans thoroughly. Transfer to a large pot and cover with water to 1 inch above surface of beans. Add salt, onion, garlic, and salt pork. Cover and simmer over medium heat until beans are tender, not mushy. Remove from heat.

In a saucepan, heat shortening and minced onions over high heat. Sauté until onions are limp and translucent. Add flour and stir until mixture turns yellow. Remove from heat and add tomato juice, salt, and pepper. Stir until lump-free.

Discard onion and garlic from beans. Ladle some beans into sauce, then stir sauce back into bean pot. Stir in brown sugar and molasses. Remove salt pork, cut into small pieces about the size of the beans, and stir pieces back in. Add Tabasco sauce. Bring mixture to a boil, stirring, then remove from heat. Let stand for at least 1 hour before serving.

SERVES 16 TO 20

DAGAR'S BEANS

Dagar's of Austin has been catering large parties for over 40 years. The company started as a barbecue business but branched out to serve just about anything anybody wants. These folks still serve lots of barbecue, though, especially during an annual June trail ride. This bean recipe serves 100, but you can cut it down if you don't have a horde to feed.

10 pounds dry pinto beans

6 tablespoons salt

1/4 cup chopped bell pepper

1 jalapeño pepper

6 tablespoons ground cumin

6 tablespoons chili powder

6 tablespoons granulated garlic

6 tablespoons paprika

4 tablespoons black pepper

Rinse beans and soak overnight in cold water. Drain, rinse, and transfer to a very large pot, then cover with fresh water. Add salt, bell pepper, and jalapeño pepper, and boil for 2 hours. Stir in remaining ingredients and turn heat down halfway. Simmer for 3 to 4 hours, stirring so beans don't stick and adding water if necessary. (*Note:* Dagar's says this recipe results in a thick, rich gravy. If you want to dress the beans up a little or make a meal out of them, add a 1-gallon can of crushed tomatoes and 5 pounds of cooked ground hamburger meat.)

SERVES 100

GENE'S TEX-MEX CROCK-POT

When you're tied up at the smoker and you don't have time to rush in and stir a pot of beans, this spicy recipe contributed by Gene Forsythe can be prepared in a Crock-Pot.

3-1/2 cups dry pinto beans

1 large onion, quartered

4 tablespoons fajita seasoning

1/4 teaspoon cayenne pepper

1/4 pound pork jowl, cubed

Rinse beans and drain thoroughly. Put all ingredients in a 3-1/2-quart Crock-Pot and cover with fresh water to 2 inches above beans. Cook on medium or low heat for 10 to 12 hours. Stir once during cooking and add 1/2 cup water if needed. Leave onion and pork jowl in beans for more flavor.

SERVES 30

GEORGETOWN VFD BEANS

More than one volunteer fire department uses an annual barbecue dinner to raise funds for equipment. When these firemen get smokin', they turn out some of the best 'que in the state.

8 pounds dry pinto beans

1 teaspoon crushed dried oregano

1 teaspoon ground cumin

1 teaspoon dried thyme

1 teaspoon garlic powder

1/2 cup salt

1/2 pound bacon, chopped

Rinse beans and soak in water overnight. Drain and rinse well, then transfer beans to a large pot. Cover with water to 1 inch above beans and then place over heat. After beans begin to simmer, add remaining ingredients. Simmer for 2 hours or until beans are tender.

SERVES 80

MAYAN RANCH BARBECUE BEANS

For over 40 years, the Mayan Ranch in Bandera, Texas, has given visitors the opportunity to be cowboys. This hill country dude ranch serves up the best of the West with old-fashioned barbecue dinners. They say this recipe isn't too sweet like baked beans, but just right for eating with brisket.

2 (23-ounce) cans ranch-style beans

1 onion, chopped and sautéed until tender

1 link Opa-brand sausage

2 tablespoons prepared mustard

1/2 cup maple syrup

1/2 cup picante sauce

Combine beans, onion, sausage, mustard, and maple syrup in a glass baking dish or pan. Top with picante sauce. Bake in a 350-degree oven for 1-1/2 hours. (*Note:* Beans can also be cooked in an iron skillet outside until onions are tender.)

SERVES 10 TO 12

BARBECUED VEGETABLES

Like your mother always said, eat your vegetables. To cook any of the follow-ing, wash and clean them first, then brush lightly with vegetable oil. Cook over medium coals and turn occasionally. How do you know if you have medium coals? Hold the palm of your hand about 4 inches above the coals and count the number of seconds you can stand the heat. With medium coals, you should be able to withstand about 4 seconds' exposure. You can make it for 5 seconds with low coals and 2 seconds with hot coals. Our thanks to the Texas Beef Industry Council for these recipes.

Bell peppers

Halve peppers lengthwise and remove seeds. Cook for 12 to 15 minutes.

Corn

Pull back husks, leaving them attached at the base and remove corn silk. Fold husks back around corn and tie at the end of the ear. Soak corn in cold water for 1 to 2 hours, then cook in smoker for 20 to 30 minutes.

Mushrooms

Select whole mushrooms, 1-3/4 to 2 inches in diameter. Cook over coals for 12 to 14 minutes.

Onions

Slice onions 1/2-inch thick. Cook until tender, about 15 or 20 minutes, turn-ing occasionally.

Potatoes

Cook or microwave small red or all-purpose white potatoes (3 to 4 ounces each) until barely tender when tested with a fork. Rinse in cold water to stop cooking, then drain well. Thread potatoes onto skewers and put in the smoker for 10 to 15 minutes.

Squash (yellow or zucchini)

Halve small squash lengthwise and cook over coals for 8 to 12 minutes.

Tomatoes

Slice tomatoes 1/2- to 3/4-inch thick. Cook over coals until heated through, about 3 to 5 minutes.

ARMADILLO EGGS

No, armadillos don't lay eggs. Still, this makes a great name for a Texas favorite. This spicy side dish was contributed by the Southfork Ranch, where exterior shots for the "Dallas" television series were filmed. You don't get much more Texan than that.

2 pounds pork sausage

3/4 pound sharp cheddar cheese, cut into 1/2-inch cubes

6 jalapeño peppers, halved and seeds removed, cut into 1/2-inch pieces

Soften sausage in a 250-degree oven for 2 to 3 minutes (do not cook). Place cheese cubes into jalapeño pieces (1 cube to each 1/2-inch slice of pepper). Roll or pat out sausage into 4-inch circles, approximately 1/4-inch thick. Wrap sausage around pepper-and-cheese bundle and shape to look like an egg. Repeat with remaining ingredients. Bake in a 350-degree oven for 12 to 15 minutes.

SERVES 6 TO 8

CAMP POTATOES

The Road Trippers, a barbecue team whose members hail from Austin, Fresno, Fairchild, Houston, and Round Top, contributed this tasty potato dish. These folks ought to know what goes well with barbecue: They've won awards for their pork, beef, and sausage at cook-offs all over the state.

3 pounds potatoes
1 large onion, sliced
1/2 pound bacon strips
2 cups grated cheddar cheese
Butter to taste
Italian dressing to taste

Wash and thinly slice potatoes (do not peel). Layer first 4 ingredients in order in an oven-safe dish. Top with pats of butter. Pour Italian dressing over mixture to moisten all ingredients. Put in a smoker and cook until potatoes are tender.

SERVES 8 TO 10

GERMAN FRIED POTATOES

This delicious side dish is the specialty of Smitty's Pit Bar-B-Que in El Paso. It's easy to make at home and adds a twist to plain potatoes.

4 medium-sized old baking potatoes (new ones don't fry up as well)

Vegetable oil

Salt to taste

Peel potatoes and quarter lengthwise. Transfer quarters to a large pan of water and boil for about 10 minutes, but do not cook until done. (Within 15 or 20 minutes, potatoes will be tender enough to pierce with fork; that's too well cooked.) Remove potatoes from hot water and drain thoroughly on paper towels. Pat dry, taking care to keep each quarter in one piece.

Heat oil in a deep skillet to 375 degrees. Fry potatoes in hot oil, doing only a few at a time if necessary to keep them far apart (do not crowd). Fry until dark golden brown, about 7 or 8 minutes. Remove potatoes from oil and drain on paper towels (keeping first batches warm on paper towels in a low oven if necessary). Season with salt and serve immediately.

SERVES 4 TO 6

MEYER'S SAUSAGE AND POTATO CASSEROLE

For over 75 years, Meyer's Elgin Sausage has been churning out beef and pork sausage, up to 35,000 pounds a week. These folks know what to do with left-over sausage. Take their hint and try this easy-to-make casserole with your favorite brand.

1-1/2 pounds Meyer's sausage, cut into 1-inch slices

4 large potatoes

1 medium onion

Salt and black pepper to taste

1/2 cup red or white wine

1 teaspoon dried parsley flakes

Brown and drain sausage. Slice potatoes and onion, and sprinkle with salt and pepper. Combine sausage, potatoes, and onion, and transfer to a deep-dish casserole. Pour wine evenly over mixture, then sprinkle with parsley flakes. Cover tightly with foil and bake in a 300-degree oven for about 1-1/2 hours. Do not uncover during baking.

SERVES 8 TO 10

SOUTHFORK'S SMOKED BAKED POTATO SALAD

J.R. may be gone from television, but he remains in the memories of Texans who make the pilgrimage to Southfork Ranch. Located north of Dallas, the ranch used for the outdoor scenes in the series is now open to the public. The restaurant there, named appropriately enough "Miss Ellie's Kitchen," serves some mighty fine barbecue, cooked in a specially designed smoker that can handle up to 200 briskets at a time. That smoker is also used to cook this flavorful potato salad, the creation of Joe "Buck" Cave, director of food and beverage for Southfork Ranch.

4 large baking potatoes

1/2 cup diced celery

1/2 cup finely chopped sweet pickles

1/2 cup chopped bell pepper

1/2 cup chopped yellow onion

1-1/2 cups salad dressing (not mayonnaise)

Salt and black pepper to taste ("Buck" recommends freshly ground pepper)

Smoke potatoes on an outdoor grill or in a smoker for 1-1/2 hours. (Mesquite or hickory wood is recommended.) Cut potatoes into 1/2- inch cubes, leaving skins on. Combine potatoes with all remaining ingredients, mixing well until everything is coated with salad dressing. Chill for at least 2 hours before serving.

SERVES 6 TO 8

GEORGETOWN VFD POTATO SALAD

Serve the troops—up to 64—at your next party with this recipe from the Georgetown Volunteer Fire Department.

10 pounds potatoes, cooked and diced (or sliced)

2 cups sweet relish

1/2 cup dill relish

2 cups chopped onion

1 cup diced pimientos

1/2 cup prepared mustard

2 quarts salad dressing

Salt and black pepper to taste

In a very large bowl, combine all ingredients, mix well, and chill. (*Note:* Quantities may be adjusted as desired for more dill or mustard taste.)

MAKES 2 GALLONS

GERMAN-STYLE POTATO SALAD

With the strong German heritage of Central Texas, it's not uncommon to find German-style rather than mayonnaise-based potato salad in many barbecue restaurants. German potato salad is vinegar-based, a hot, tart blend of flavors that make a good complement to barbecue. This recipe comes from Paris's mother, Carlene Permenter, who prepares the dish with barbecue and also with holiday meals.

5 pounds potatoes, washed and peeled

1 large white onion, diced

3 large kosher dill pickles, diced

1 small jar pimientos, drained

1/2 cup white vinegar or pickle juice, or a combination

Salt and black pepper to taste

Quarter potatoes and boil until soft. Rinse potatoes and mash until chunky. Add onion, pickles, pimientos, and vinegar. Mix ingredients well. Season with salt and pepper (use pepper generously). Serve hot or cold.

SERVES 6 TO 8

RUDY MIKESKA'S COLESLAW

The Mikeska family is known throughout Texas for their barbecue. With restaurants scattered across the state, folks from Columbus to El Campo and from Taylor to Temple have had the chance to sample the Mikeskas' work. This recipe comes from Rudy Mikeska's in Taylor, courtesy of CEO Tim Mikeska. "We've got secret recipes, and we've got not-so-secret recipes. We've found, though, that even if you get the recipe down to the very grain, it will taste different than it does in our restaurants. It may be the pots or whatever, but it's a little different."

This recipe may taste a little different than it does at Rudy Mikeska's, but it's still mighty good. This same slaw was served recently at the company's largest catered event, with over 21,000 guests (that's over 4,000 pounds of coleslaw!). Tim has reduced the recipe here to a manageable size.

6 good-sized heads green cabbage

1 head purple cabbage

4 peeled carrots

3 bell peppers, cored

2 stalks of celery (tops removed)

1 to 2 pounds sugar, to taste

6 to 12 tablespoons black pepper, to taste

3/4 cup red wine vinegar, or to taste

1/2 to 1 gallon Miracle Whip salad dressing

Remove all loose leaves from green cabbage heads, then shred or chop remainder to a consistent size. Shred or grate purple cabbage and carrots. Finely grind bell pepper and celery, and mix together. In a very large bowl, combine all of these prepared ingredients, then stir in sugar and red wine vinegar. (Add each seasoning carefully to taste.) Fold in salad dressing. Serve thoroughly chilled.

SERVES ABOUT 35

BBQ CORN SALAD

The chef of the Hyatt Hill Country Resort prepares this Southwestern-style barbecue salad in the restaurant as well as for catered events at the sprawling resort northwest of San Antonio.

10 husked ears of corn

2 cups corn oil

3 cups barbecue sauce (your choice)

2 red bell peppers, diced small

2 green bell peppers, diced small

1 red onion, diced small

1 pound cactus leaves, julienned

1/4 cup fresh lime juice

1 tablespoon chopped garlic

1/4 cup balsamic vinegar

2 bunches cilantro, chopped

Cook corn by first rubbing it with 1-3/4 cups corn oil and then placing it on a prepared grill over charcoal or mesquite. While corn is cooking to a golden brown, baste with up to 2 cups barbecue sauce and turn continuously to avoid burning. Remove corn from grill and allow to cool.

In a large bowl, combine bell peppers, onion, cactus leaves, lime juice, and garlic. When corn has cooled, remove kernels from each cob with a knife. Add corn to bell pepper mixture and stir in remaining 1/4 cup corn oil, balsamic vinegar, chopped cilantro, and remaining 1 cup barbecue sauce. Chill and serve.

SERVES 16 TO 20

CHEESY LOAF

Prepare this simple creation from the National Pork Producers in your smoker just before serving the meal.

1 loaf **French bread, sliced not quite completely through**

1/2 cup (1 stick) **butter, softened**

2 tablespoons **minced parsley**

1/2 cup **grated Parmesan cheese or crumbled blue cheese**

Mix butter with parsley and cheese, and spread between slices of French bread. Wrap loaf in foil and place in cooker (not over direct coals) for 10 to 12 minutes.

SERVES 8

GUADALUPE MUD CAKE

The Guadalupe Smoked Meat Company in the historic community of Gruene tempts diners with this unbeatable dessert.

1 cup (2 sticks) margarine

2 cups sugar

1/3 cup cocoa

4 eggs

1 teaspoon vanilla extract

1-1/2 cups all-purpose flour

1 cup chopped pecans

Dash of salt

1 (8-ounce) jar marshmallow creme

ICING

1/2 cup (1 stick) margarine

1/2 cup milk

1 teaspoon vanilla extract

1 box powdered sugar

1/2 cup cocoa

1/4 cup chopped pecans

For cake, first cream margarine, sugar, and cocoa, then add eggs and vanilla. Mix well, then add flour, pecans, and salt. Beat for 2 minutes until blended. Pour batter into a 9-by-13-inch greased sheet-cake pan and bake at 350 degrees for 35 minutes.

When cake is done, spread hot cake with marshmallow creme and set aside to cool.

To make icing, melt margarine in a saucepan and then add milk and vanilla. Stir in powdered sugar and cocoa until smooth. Spread mixture over marshmallow creme, then sprinkle pecans on top.

SERVES 10 TO 12

NEW BRAUNFELS SMOKEHOUSE BREAD PUDDING

Since 1945 this little smokehouse has been churning out spicy sausage. The folks here know that sausage and barbecue plates can sizzle the taste buds and send some diners grabbing for a giant glass of iced tea. Here at the New Braunfels Smokehouse barbecue lovers can relax and pour on extra sauce (or throw caution to the wind and eat a jalapeño on the side), knowing that this dessert will cool the burn.

4 eggs

1 cup sugar

2 teaspoons vanilla extract

4 cups milk

1-1/2 loaves white bread, cubed

6 tablespoons raisins

1/2 cup firmly packed brown
    sugar

BUTTER SAUCE

3/4 cup sugar

3 egg yolks, beaten

3 tablespoons melted butter

2 tablespoons cornstarch
    dissolved in 1/4 cup water

1-1/2 cups boiling water

2 teaspoons vanilla extract

1/8 teaspoon salt

In a bowl, beat together eggs and sugar. Add vanilla and milk, and beat again. Stir in bread and raisins. Divide mixture between two greased 9-by-9-by-2-inch loaf pans. Sprinkle the top of each with 1/4 cup brown sugar. Bake at 350 degrees for 30 minutes or until pudding has risen to top of pan.

To make sauce, cream sugar, eggs, and butter in a double boiler. Stir in cornstarch mixture, then slowly add boiling water. Cook over hot water until thickened, stirring constantly. Add vanilla and salt, then remove from heat.

Serve pudding warm, topped with warm butter sauce.

SERVES 8

BANANA PUDDING

This favorite Texas dessert is a staple at all barbecue restaurants. Lois Null contributed this easy-to-prepare recipe.

6 eggs, beaten

2 cups sugar

2 cups all-purpose flour

2-1/2 to 3 cups milk

2 teaspoons vanilla extract

1/2 box vanilla wafers

6 sliced bananas

In a saucepan, combine eggs, sugar, flour, and milk, and cook over low heat until mixture thickens. Remove from heat and add vanilla extract, stirring until blended. Set aside to cool.

Line a rectangular serving dish with half the vanilla wafers and half the sliced bananas. Top with half the pudding, then repeat layering of wafers and bananas. Spoon in remaining pudding and refrigerate until ready to serve.

SERVES 6 TO 8

PEACH COBBLER

This tasty dessert, contributed by the Texas Department of Agriculture, uses one of the state's best products: tasty peaches. If you're looking for peaches straight from the tree, swing through the hill country town of Stonewall in early summer.

1 egg

1 cup sugar

3 tablespoons melted shortening or butter

1/3 cup milk

Grated zest of 1 lemon

1 cup all-purpose flour

2 teaspoons baking powder

1/2 teaspoon salt

8 fresh peaches, peeled and sliced

1 tablespoon fresh lemon juice

1 teaspoon ground cinnamon or 1/2 teaspoon ground nutmeg

Whipped cream or ice cream

Beat together egg, 1/4 cup sugar, shortening, milk, and lemon zest. Sift flour, baking powder, and salt into egg mixture and beat thoroughly. Half fill a greased 9-by-12-inch baking dish with peaches and sprinkle with lemon juice. Combine remaining sugar with spice and sprinkle over peaches. Cover with batter and bake at 375 degrees for 30 minutes. Served hot or cold, with whipped cream or ice cream.

SERVES 6 TO 8

TEXAS PECAN PIE

No barbecue menu would be complete without a homemade pecan pie. The recipe for this sweet temptation comes from the Muldoon Home Demonstration Club.

9-inch unbaked pie shell

1 cup dark corn syrup

1/2 cup sugar

3 eggs

1 cup whole pecans

1 teaspoon vanilla extract

Pinch of salt

2 tablespoons melted butter

In a bowl, combine corn syrup, sugar, eggs, pecans, vanilla, salt, and melted butter. Pour into pie shell and bake in a 350-degree oven for 30 to 40 minutes, until golden brown.

SERVES 6 TO 8

COOK-OFFS AND FESTIVALS

From the Panhandle to the Piney Woods, from Gulf beaches to the Mexican border, Texas is dotted with barbecue cook-offs. The pits usually fire up on Friday afternoons and contestants stay up through the night, checking their meats to make sure they reach smoky perfection. Judging is generally mid-day on Saturday, and afterwards most cook-offs invite the public to wander among the contestants and judge the barbecue for themselves. How do you judge good barbecue from a so-so product? Typically judges base their decisions on color and appearance (especially a well-defined smoke ring), texture, taste, and aroma.

Some cook-offs are as ephemeral as the smoke they produce; if you are entering, contact the sponsors well in advance in case of changes. We've tried to select long-running competitions here, but nonetheless plan to make your entry as soon as possible in case the dates have changed.

JANUARY

TROY VOLUNTEER FIRE DEPARTMENT
P.O. Box 1, Troy, TX 76579. (817) 938-2188
Stay warm near the pits during this fire department cook-off featuring beans, chili, chicken, and pork north of Temple on I-35.

FEBRUARY

JACK-O-LOPE BBQ AND CHILI COOKOFF
North Texas Fairgrounds, 2306 Bolivar, Denton, TX 76201-0835.
(817) 387-1677
Bring out your best brisket, ribs, chicken, or jackpot beans at this north Texas cook-off. Keep an eye out for the legendary jack-o-lope, that Texas combination of antelope and jackrabbit that lives only on souvenir postcards.

LIVESTOCK AND RODEO SHOW BARBECUE COOK OFF
P.O. Box 20070, Houston, TX 77225. (713) 791-9000

The world's largest stock show includes country and western entertainment, parades, rodeos, and a barbecue cook-off with over 100 contestants. Trophies are awarded for best chicken, ribs, brisket, and overall winner, as well as for "Most Colorful Team or Contestant," "Cleanest Contestant Area," "Most Unique Pit," and "Best Skit." Write for a copy of the four-page rules with details on mandatory insurance for each contestant or team.

MARCH

AUSTIN–TRAVIS COUNTY LIVESTOCK SHOW AND RODEO
c/o Judi Ford, 7600 Chevy Chase Dr., Ste. 101, Austin, TX 78752

This mid-March rodeo is one of Austin's biggest events, featuring national country and western performers and rodeo action to bring out the Texan in everyone. And what's Texas without barbecue? No need to find out because there's plenty here at the Barbecue Cook- Off. There's only one category: brisket or beef clod.

GENERAL GRANBURY'S BIRTHDAY PARTY AND BEAN COOK-OFF
Granbury Convention and Visitors Bureau, 100 N. Crockett, Granbury, TX 76048. (800) 950-2212

This mid-March cook-off near Fort Worth celebrates the birthday of Civil War hero Hiram Granbury when 50 contestants vie for "best beans," "best ribs," and "best decorated entry." There are also bean and rib eating contests, outhouse races around the Hood County Courthouse, Indian dancers, cloggers, and musicians.

KIKM BAR-B-QUE AND CHILI COOKOFF
c/o Jim Vandergriff, P.O. Box 1362, Sherman, TX 75091. (903) 893-3391

This North Texas cook-off selects the best pork ribs, brisket, jackpot beans, and chicken, as well as chili.

MONTGOMERY COUNTY BARBECUE COOKOFF
P.O. Box 869, Conroe, TX 77305

Over 100 teams compete in this invitational barbecue festival near Houston. Held the fourth weekend in March, the cook-off is the culmination of a week-long fair, complete with a rodeo and carnival.

APRIL

FIREMEN'S EXTRAVAGANZA
Elgin Volunteer Fire Department, Elgin, TX 78621. (512) 285-4515
(Chamber of Commerce)
The capital of Texas sausage making throws this cook-off the first weekend in April with cash prizes for brisket, pork ribs, chicken, game, jackpot beans, showmanship, master cook, and best rig.

LIBERTY HILL VFW POST 8200 COOKOFF
BBQ Chairperson, VFW Post 8200, Liberty Hill, TX 78642.
(512) 778-6913
Located northwest of Austin, Liberty Hill hosts this cook-off to select best brisket, pork, exotic meats, sausage, and jackpot beans.

LION'S CLUB BARBECUE COOKOFF
1028 Alma, Lumberton, TX 77656. (409) 755-4542
Just north of Beaumont, this town of 2,000 turns out to enjoy this free brisket cook-off every April. Don't look for crowds either from diners or cookers; there are only about 15 contestants every year. This is a chance to enjoy a real small-town cook-off.

LLANO COUNTY CHAMBER OF COMMERCE BBQ COOKOFF
700 Bessemer, Llano, TX 78643. (915) 247-5354
The deer-hunting capital of Texas hosts a beef and pork cook-off on the banks of the Llano River in late April. An arts and crafts fair and a flea market are held in conjunction with the hill country event.

SPRINGFEST AND BARBECUE COOKOFF
403 N. Main St., Cleburne, TX 76031
This cook-off south of Fort Worth gives awards for best brisket, chicken, beans, and ribs, plus a prize to the entrant who traveled the farthest distance. Folks enjoy a horseshoe pitchin' tournament and a street dance as part of the festivities.

TEXAS STATE CHAMPIONSHIP FIDDLER'S FROLICS
Knights of Columbus Hall, P.O. Box 46, Hallettsville, TX 77964.
(512) 798-2311
On the fourth weekend in April, listen to championship fiddlers and guitar pickers while you enjoy the fruits of the barbecue and barbecue sauce cook-offs. Hallettsville is north of Victoria on US 77.

WEST TEXAS CHAMPIONSHIP BAR-B-QUE AND CHILI COOK-OFF
Sonora Chamber of Commerce, Sonora, TX 76950. (915) 387-2880
This twin cook-off takes place west of the Texas hill country in the town that's best known as the home of the Caverns of Sonora. Held the second weekend in April, the contest features brisket and chicken. There's also a "Jack-Pot Goat Cook-Off" where contestants can try out their best barbecued goat recipe.

WURST COOK-OFF AND DANCE
P.O. Box 310309, New Braunfels, TX 78131-0309. (800) 221-4369
This late April festival celebrates spring in Landa Park. Up to 40 teams compete in the cook-off for best brisket, pork ribs, chicken, and side dishes.

MAY

COW CAMP COOKOFF
San Saba Chamber of Commerce, San Saba, TX 76887. (915) 372-5141
Fire up the pit and pull out your best brisket, pork ribs, or chicken recipe to compete for more than $2,000 in prizes. San Saba, "The Pecan Capital of the World," celebrates this hill country cook-off with plenty of pecan pies followed by volleyball, horseshoes and washers, and an antique and classic car show.

KIMBLE COUNTY COOK-OFF
Kimble County Chamber of Commerce, 402 Main St., Junction, TX 76849. (915) 446-3190
On the South Llano River in the western hill country, competitors fire up their pits in late May for prizes in brisket, chicken, goat, pork ribs, chili, beans, corn bread, and margaritas.

STAGECOACH BBQ COOKOFF
Chamber of Commerce, P.O. Box 520, Marshall, TX 75671. (903) 935-7868
The East Texas town of Marshall hosts this cook-off on the third weekend in May with plenty of barbecue at the Civic Center plus arts and crafts, a street dance, and live entertainment.

SUMMER FUN FEST EXPO AND BENEFIT
Collin County Youth Park, Rt. 4, Box 149C, McKinney, TX 75070
Jackpot beans, half chicken, pork ribs, brisket, and outlaw chili titles are up for grabs at this summer cook-off located north of Dallas.

JUNE

BARBECUE COOKOFF AND STREET DANCE
P.O. Box 1230, Temple, TX 76503. (817) 773-5252

Temple celebrates the last weekend in June with an old-fashioned street dance and a free barbecue cook-off. Competition takes place in chicken, beef (shoulder clod or brisket), and pork categories, and awards also are given for best showmanship and best pit. Sponsored by the local radio station, this cook-off has been operating over a decade and a half with arts and crafts and live entertainment on hand.

CHISHOLM TRAIL ROUNDUP BARBECUE COOKOFF
Chamber of Commerce, P.O. Drawer 840, Lockhart, TX 78644. (512) 398-2818

The "Barbecue Capital of Texas" fires up the pits in mid-June for this cook-off. It is part of a festival celebrating the days when Lockhart was the southern collection point for the Chisholm Trail.

CHISHOLM TRAIL ROUNDUP, TRAILBLAZER X BBQ COOK-OFF
P.O. Box 4815, Ft. Worth, TX 76164-0815. (800) 433-5747

The second weekend in June, Fort Worth celebrates its history as the last major stop on the legendary Chisholm Trail with this festival in the Stockyards District. Over 60 teams compete in the categories of beef, beans, pork spareribs, and chicken. The grand champion advances to the National Cook-Offs. Besides the cook-off, Fort Worth parties with a trail ride, shootouts, street dances, and a professional rodeo.

COLLIN PARK BARBECUE COOK-OFF
c/o Joe Castro, P.O. Box 1177, Wylie, TX 75098. (214) 442-5755

Head east of Dallas to the shores of Lake Lavon to taste superior jackpot beans, half chicken, pork ribs, and brisket. The park has a boat ramp, RV hookups, a beach, and volleyball courts.

CORN FESTIVAL
City of Holland, P.O. Box 157, Holland, TX 76534. (817) 657-2460

This small town, one hour northeast of Austin, celebrates the corn harvest with a corncob-throwing contest and a barbecue cook-off featuring brisket, ribs, chicken, and exotic categories.

FT. TRAILS SHRINE CLUB ANNUAL BARBECUE COOKOFF
c/o Angie Sprickland, P.O. Box 680, Jacksboro, TX 76458.
(817) 567-5134

Part of the Old Mesquiteville Festival on the courthouse square, this cook-off features half chicken, pork ribs, and brisket. There's also an art show and horseshoe tournament. Jacksboro is located northwest of Fort Worth.

LLANO CHAMBER OF COMMERCE BBQ COOK-OFF
700 Bessemer, Llano, TX 78643. (915) 247-5354

Llano gets smokin' with competition in chicken, pork brisket, sausage, goat, and showmanship.

NORTH TEXAS AREA BBQ COOKERS ASSOCIATION ANNUAL COOKOFF
North Texas Fairgrounds, P.O. Box 3024, Denton, TX 76201

The grand champion at this cook-off qualifies for an invitation to the Kansas City Barbeque Society, Jack Daniel Invitational, and Meridian National Championship cook-offs. The late June competition includes brisket, half chicken, and open pork ribs. Young smokers can compete in the Junior National Championship Cookoff here as well.

TOM TOM FESTIVAL AND RODEO
Yoakum Chamber of Commerce, P.O. Box 591, Yoakum, TX 77995.
(512) 293-2309

Yoakum, located northwest of Victoria, is the "Leather Capital of the World." Leather means cattle, cattle means beef, and, in these parts, beef means barbecue. Enjoy this cook-off the weekend of the first Saturday in June, with activities Thursday through Saturday.

JULY

FIREMAN'S FIELD DAY
c/o Mike Garner, 303 Perking Rd., Aubrey, TX 76227

Chicken, pork ribs, brisket, and chili are the categories in this fiery cook-off. Aubrey is located east of Denton in North Texas.

4TH OF JULY CELEBRATION BBQ COOKOFF AND FIREWORKS CELEBRATION
Chamber of Commerce, P.O. Box 97, Terrell, TX 75160. (214) 563-5703

Pit and backyard cooker categories include brisket, ribs, and chicken as well as beans and cobbler in this cook-off held east of Dallas.

4TH OF JULY COOKOFF
c/o D. L. Johnson, P.O. Box 9135, Corpus Christi, TX 78469.
(800) 678-6232 (Convention and Visitors Bureau)
Benefiting the Special Olympics, this patriotic cook-off is smokin' with brisket, ribs, fajitas, and chicken.

THE GREAT MOSQUITO FESTIVAL
Parks and Recreation Dept., P.O. Box 997, Clute, TX 77531.
(409) 265-8392
See the crowning of Ms. Quito, the "Skeeter Beeter" baby crawling contest, and the mosquito legs look-alike contest before you sample the results of the barbecue and fajita cook-offs. Don't worry, the smoke from the pits will probably keep the mosquitoes away from this Gulf coast community, at least for this weekend in late July.

SPRING HO FESTIVAL
Lampasas Chamber of Commerce, Santa Fe Railroad Depot,
P.O. Box 627, 501 E. Second St., Lampasas, TX 76550. (512) 556-5172
This hill country festival features the most summertime of activities: a street dance, washer pitchin' contests, a kids' fishing derby, and, of course, a barbecue cook-off featuring chicken, brisket, pork, and exotics.

TEXAS STATE CHAMPIONSHIP COOKOFF (BIG SPRING)
HC 71, Box 55A, Coahoma, TX 79511. (915) 965-3491
The winners of this cook-off go on to the American Royal in Kansas City and the Lynchburg, Tennessee, American Championship Cookoff. Open to all competitors, the categories are brisket, pork spareribs, half whole chicken, and pork loin. There are also prizes given for showmanship and best pit, judged not to be the fanciest pit, but the one that is most serviceable and usable. Competitors can spread out on the Big Spring golf course and take up as much room as they like. The cook-off is always held the third weekend in July.

TOWN AND COUNTRY JAMBOREE
Chamber of Commerce, P.O. Box 482, Moulton, TX 77975.
(512) 596-7205
Pull out your best recipes for pork butt, brisket, and pinto beans for this small-town cook-off between San Antonio and Houston.

WATERMELON FESTIVAL
Hempstead Chamber of Commerce, P.O. Drawer 517, Hempstead, TX 77445-0518. (409) 826-8217 or 826-4127

Watch the coronation of the Watermelon Festival Queen then pig out on barbecue at the cook-off held the third Saturday in July. Hempstead, the "Watermelon Capital of the World," is west of Houston on US 290. The town celebrates the harvest with arts and crafts, entertainment, and a cook-off featuring brisket and pork ribs. Prizes also are awarded for showmanship.

AUGUST

ALIEF SOUTHWEST RODEO FEST BBQ AND CHILI COOKOFF
25 Thornhill Oaks, Houston, TX 77015

A benefit for the Houston Livestock Show and Rodeo School, this cook-off includes brisket, ribs, sausage, chicken, and chili judging. After sampling some barbecue, try your hand at horseshoe pitching, washer tossing, and hay hauling.

DEAD COW COOKIN' AND BEAN FIXIN' EXTRAVAGANZA
Maskat Temple, P.O. Box 1950, Wichita Falls, TX 76307. (817) 766-4511

This cook-off benefits the Shriner's Hospital for Crippled Children. Up to 75 teams can compete for prizes in brisket, ribs, beans, and chicken at this early August event.

HITCHCOCK GOOD OLE DAYS
Hitchcock Chamber of Commerce, P.O. Box 389, Hitchcock, TX 77563. (409) 986-9224

Sponsored by the Chamber of Commerce, this mid-August event near Galveston awards cash and trophies to best ribs, brisket, and beans, with first and second place trophies for showmanship.

INTERNATIONAL BARBECUE COOKOFF
P.O. Box 230, Taylor, TX 76574. (512) 352-6364

They come from around the state to compete here in seven categories. Over 100 teams roll into Taylor's Murphy Park and enjoy two days of pit partying. Besides the usual offerings, you'll also find teams here preparing kingfish, rabbit, venison, rattlesnake (yes, it does taste like chicken), and even raccoon (no, it's not like chicken, but more like a slightly sweet brisket). The categories include pork, beef, poultry, goat, lamb, wild game, and seafood. The grand champion qualifies for the Kansas City Barbeque Society American Royal invitational and the Jack Daniel invitational in Lynchburg.

NATIONAL CHAMPIONSHIP BARBECUE COOKOFF
P.O. Box 699, Meridian, TX 76665. (817) 435-6113

This serious cook-off is by invitation only with thousands of dollars in prize money up for grabs. To enter, you must have placed in a recognized cook-off. Contestants choose from numerous categories, including pork ribs, pork other than ribs, brisket, chicken breast, pinto beans, showmanship, best rig, and best layout. The event is always the last Saturday in August. Meridian is located northeast of Waco.

NORTH TEXAS STATE FAIR ASSOCIATION BARBECUE COOKOFF
Denton, TX 76202. (817) 387-2632

Chicken, ribs, beans, and brisket are on the smoker at this cook-off.

XIT RODEO AND REUNION
P.O. Box 966, Dalhart, TX 79022. (800) 249-5646
(Chamber of Commerce)

This event honors the now dwindling number of ranch hands who once worked the XIT (Ten in Texas) Ranch about 60 miles northwest of Amarillo. There's no cook-off here, but this early August festival holds what it calls the world's largest free barbecue feed on the world's largest fenced-in ranch. Who can turn down free barbecue?

SEPTEMBER

BARNIE McBEE MEMORIAL BBQ COOKOFF
Chamber of Commerce, P.O. Box 65, Comanche, TX 76442.
(915) 356-3233

This cook-off in north Central Texas is part of the Comanche County Pow-wow Festival held the last weekend of September, with recognition given for best beef brisket, pork ribs, half chicken, jackpot beans, and showmanship. There is also a carnival, an arts and crafts show, and Indian dances held in conjunction with the festival.

BARTLETT VOLUNTEER FIRE DEPARTMENT BBQ COOK-OFF
P.O. Box 579, Bartlett, TX 76511. (817) 527-3333

Try your hand in the pork, brisket, chicken, and exotic categories. This small town located halfway between Austin and Temple holds its cook-off the last Saturday of September.

CHILI SUPERBOWL COOKOFF
Convention and Visitors Bureau, P.O. Box 2281, 325 Hickory St., Abilene, TX 79604. (915) 677-2781

Held Labor Day weekend at the Buffalo Gap Perini Ranch, this chili cook-off also features a brisket cook-off.

COCKROACH FESTIVAL AND BARBECUE FESTIVAL
Fraternal Order of Eagles, 6101 FM 646 S., Santa Fe, TX 77510

Cash prizes await the teams here with the best brisket, pork ribs, and beans during the third weekend in September. The festival, held between Houston and Galveston, also features horse rides, arts and crafts, and musical entertainment.

COUNTY FAIR AND BARBECUE COOKOFF
Magnolia Area Chamber of Commerce, P.O. Box 399, Magnolia, TX 77355. (713) 356-1488

Held the third weekend in September, this cook-off is judged by local sheriffs. There's also a car show, games, the crowning of Miss Magnolia, and a dance the night before the cookout. Magnolia is northwest of Houston.

GARWOOD RICE FESTIVAL BBQ COOK-OFF
Garwood Community Association, c/o Gay Stephens, P.O. Box 244, Garwood, TX 77442

Located southwest of Houston, this late September cook-off is open to all competitors. It starts with a Friday night party for all cooks and workers, who then tend their meats and prepare for Saturday's judging of best brisket, chicken, rice, beans, and chili.

JUMPIN' JACK JAMBOREE
Chamber of Commerce, P.O. Box 1528, Azle, TX 76098. (817) 444-1143

Located 23 miles northwest of Arlington, Azle puts on a show in late September on Main Street with musical entertainment, a children's area, an arts and crafts show, a bike tour, and a cook-off with prizes for brisket and showmanship.

LAKE THOMAS BBQ AND CHILI COOK-OFF
HC 71, Box 55A, Coahoma, TX 79511

Held at West Texas's Lake Thomas on the last weekend in September, this cook-off features chicken, ribs, brisket, beans, chili, and junior chili categories.

RIB TICKLIN' AFFAIR
Austin, TX. (512) 440-4036

This late September festival takes place at Auditorium Shores on the banks of Town Lake. It's held to benefit the Austin–Travis County Mental Health Mental Retardation Center. The competition for "best ribs" is only open to teams and restaurants selected by Travis County MHMR, but there's lots of good eating for the general public to enjoy.

SAM BASS BAR-B-QUE COOKOFF
Round Rock Police Officers Association, 615 E. Palm Valley Blvd., Round Rock, TX 78664. (512) 218-5500, ext. 12 or 15

Held in Round Rock's Old Settlers Park, this cook-off has teams from around the state vying for thousands of dollars in prize money in categories that include brisket, chicken, pork ribs, wild game, seafood, beans, best rig, master cook, and showmanship.

SANGER HERITAGE SELLEBRATION AND TEXAS STATE CHAMPIONSHIP BBQ COOK-OFF
Sanger Chamber of Commerce, Sanger, TX 76266. (817) 458-7702

Always the second Saturday in September, this North Texas barbecue cook-off features brisket, pork ribs, chicken, and beans as competitors vie for generous cash prizes. When you're tired of eating, walk over and look at the arts and crafts at the Sellebration. Admission is free.

TOMATO FEST BARBECUE COOKOFF
Jacksonville Chamber of Commerce, P.O. Box 1231, Jacksonville, TX 75766. (903) 586-2217

Tomatoes are an important part of Texas barbecue sauces, so it's natural that the Tomato Fest includes a cook-off. Prizes are awarded for brisket, pork ribs, chicken, exotic game, and barbecue sauce. Besides the cook-off, the Fest features crafts, volleyball, horseshoes and washers, and even "The Battle of San Tomato." Wear old clothes to this one, located south of Tyler in East Texas.

WORLD CHAMPIONSHIP BARBECUED GOAT COOKOFF
Brady Chamber of Commerce, 101 E. First St., Brady, TX 76825. (915) 597-2420

Usually held the Saturday before Labor Day, this cook-off brings in as many as 125 competitors to west Central Texas. Goat or cabrito is the order of the day here. After a lunch of cabrito, watch a sheep dog–handling contest, a goat pill flip off, or a tobacco spittin' contest.

WORLD CHAMPIONSHIP BAR-B-QUE BEEF COOK-OFF
**Pecos Chamber of Commerce, P.O. Box 27, Pecos, TX 79772.
(915) 445-2406**

This fall festival, held in conjunction with the county fall fair, livestock show, and concert, is the largest in West Texas. Scheduled for the last weekend in September, the barbecue cook-off attracts up to 75 brisket cooks. Unlike most competitions, here officials provide all the meat.

OCTOBER

ANNUAL COLLEYVILLE BBQ COOK-OFF
**Chamber of Commerce, P.O. Box 69, Colleyville, TX 76034.
(817) 488-7148**

Compete for trophies and cash prizes in this cook-off that features brisket, ribs, chicken, and beans. There's a pancake breakfast for cooks on Saturday. Colleyville is located between Fort Worth and Dallas.

BBQ CHILI COOKOFF
**Elks Lodge #2280, Sherman, TX 75090. (903) 893-1184
(Chamber of Commerce)**

Proceeds from this North Texas cook-off go the the Texas Elks Service Center for Handicapped Children. This late October event has categories in beef, pork, chicken, and beans.

CZHILISPIEL
**Flatonia Chamber of Commerce, P.O. Box 651, Flatonia, TX 78941.
(512) 865-3920**

Held the last full weekend in October, this festival located between San Antonio and Houston is one of the largest chili cook-offs in Texas, with over 200 teams. Barbecue is well represented here, too.

DENTON COUNTY LIVESTOCK ASSOCIATION AND YOUTH FAIR BBQ COOK-OFF
**Denton Chamber of Commerce, P.O. Drawer P, Denton, TX
76202-1719. (817) 382-7895**

This mid-October cook-off is held at the North Texas Fairgrounds. It's an event sanctioned by the North Texas Area Barbecue Cookers Association (see Appendix C: Barbecue Associations and Publications).

GAINESVILLE ANTIQUE CAR CLUB BBQ COOK-OFF
Rt. 6, Box 462, Gainesville, TX 76240. (817) 665-2512 (Brad Scott)

It's cars and 'que at this North Texas cook-off held the first weekend in October. There are prizes awarded for best chicken, brisket, pork ribs, and beans, as well as for best pit.

HARRIS COUNTY FAIR BBQ COOK-OFF
1 Abercrombie Dr., Houston, TX 77084. (713) 463-6650

Sponsored by the Houston Farm and Ranch Club, this cook-off includes awards for best chicken, pork ribs, beans, brisket, most congenial cook, best showmanship, cleanest area, and even aluminum can recycling! The admission fee for the cook-off includes admission to the county fair. This cook-off is always the last full weekend in October.

INTERNATIONAL BBQ COOKERS ASSOCIATION (IBCA) JACKPOT CHAMPIONSHIP, IBCA INVITATIONAL COOKOFF, AND BRINKMANN BACKYARDER BBQ COOK OFF
Traders Village, 2602 Mayfield Rd., Grand Prairie, TX 75051. (214) 647-2331

There's something for every barbecue chef at this cook-off that bills itself as the second largest in Texas. The Brinkmann cook-off draws backyard cookers, and the International BBQ Cookers Association is for the big guns with customized trailered smokers. The whole show takes place at Traders Village, one of the largest flea markets in Texas, located between Dallas and Fort Worth. Every weekend, 1,600 dealers fill the 106-acre park.

KELLER WILD WEST DAYS
City of Keller, P.O. Box 1422, Keller, TX 76248. (817) 431-2169

Primitive (pre-1850) cooking only is allowed at this cook-off, with categories in meat, vegetables, and dessert. Keller is north of Fort Worth.

LICKSKILLET FESTIVAL
P.O. Box 217, Fayetteville, TX 78940. (409) 378-2311

You'll feel like licking the skillet after a taste of the barbecue at this south Central Texas cook-off on the third weekend in October.

PARKFEST IN TEAGUE
Teague Chamber of Commerce, 1010 E. Loop 255, Teague, TX 75860. (817) 739-2061

Jackpot beans, chicken, ribs, brisket, and showmanship categories draw competitors to this small town east of Mexia. The cook-off is primarily a local competition, with one pitmaster challenging another. Besides the cook-off there are arts and crafts, games, and food booths.

POWDER PUFF COOKOFF, LADIES ONLY
Conroe Elks Lodge, Rt. 4, Box 736, Conroe, TX 77302. (409) 231-3557

Holy smokes—competitors can have no male assistance in this ladies-only competition held north of Houston. Categories include beef, ribs, chicken, chili, beans, salad, and even Bloody Marys.

SASSAFRAS FESTIVAL
Chamber of Commerce, 611 W. Columbia, San Augustine, TX 75972. (409) 275-3610

This east Texas town located 38 miles west of Nacogdoches celebrates with arts and crafts, live entertainment, and a barbecue cook-off featuring beef, pork, poultry, and beans. Admission is free. Cook-off participants are requested to give out samples, but they may also sell barbecue following the judging.

STATE FAIR RIB ROUNDUP AND CHILI COOKOFF
Fair Park, P.O. Box 26010, Dallas, TX 75226. (214) 421-8713 or 421-8744

Spanning almost the entire month of October, the state fair of Texas is one of the largest expositions in the country.

WILD WEST POSSUM FEST BBQ COOK-OFF
Graham Chamber of Commerce, Graham, TX 76450. (800) 256-4844

Compete in jackpot beans (dry pintos only), half fully jointed chicken, pork spareribs, or beef brisket categories at this early October cook-off in North Texas. Save time to watch the turtle races or to shop for arts and crafts.

WURSTFEST
New Braunfels Chamber of Commerce, P.O. Box 311417, New Braunfels, TX 78131-1417. (800) 572-2626

From late October through early November, sample some of the best of Texas's sausage at this celebration of sausage making. There's no cook-off here, just one of the largest German celebrations in the country and the chance to enjoy sausage, beer, and music.

APPENDIX B
BARBECUE GIFTS AND PRODUCTS

OK, you can't put Texas in a bottle. But you can take home a little Lone Star flavor in the form of a bottle of barbecue sauce, a gift basket of sausage, or a bag of mesquite wood chips. Some restaurants have even gone high tech and linked up with overnight delivery services to bring your favorite brisket or ribs right to your door, wherever that door may be.

Barbecue sauces make great presents, easy to wrap and ship. And what better way to share the spicy, tangy taste of Texas barbecue? It may not be quite as good as sitting with your hands wrapped around a rib in a hot, smoke-filled barbecue joint, lit by a few neon beer signs, but you can pretend. Run down to the grocery store and buy a six-pack of cold Lone Star, Pearl, or Shiner, slip on some boots, fire up the pit, replace the dishes with brown butcher paper, get out the sauce, and dig in.

SAUCES

AUSTIN'S OWN BBQ SAUCE
P.O. Box 200395, Austin, TX 78720-0395. (512) 219-1960
or fax (512) 219-1961

Take your pick: original, hot, and hotter. Austin's Own has them all. The spicy concoction is called Austin's Own Border Edition. Fire eaters will want to order Austin's Own Olé Chipotle, a smoked jalapeño barbecue sauce.

CATTLEBARON FOODS, INC.
P.O. Drawer 800037, Dallas, TX 75380. (800) 357-9106

Cattlebaron makes a whole line of retail products including marinades for beef and chicken and three varieties of barbecue sauce: traditional, mesquite, and jalapeño. The company also makes a line of specialty products sold under the name Texas Originals that includes several barbecue sauces, marinades, and picante sauces.

CLAUDE'S SAUCES, INC.
935 Loma Verde, El Paso, TX 79936. (800) 72-SAUCE
Claude's was founded by Claude Struve, a grocery store butcher who originally sold brisket at the Cincinnati Street Market in El Paso. Claude's secret was his marinating sauce, and some said his use of papaya juice in the marinade as a natural meat tenderizer was the key. Today Claude has retired, but the secret sauces are still sold by Joe and Glenda Castañeda. The company manufactures six sauces, including Claude's Barbecue Brisket Sauce, a tomato-based barbecue sauce, a fajita marinade, and others.

DICKEY'S BARBECUE SAUCE
Dickey's BBQ Pits, 4610 N. Central, Dallas, TX 75230. (214) 823-0240
Since 1941 Dickey's BBQ Pits restaurants in the Dallas–Fort Worth area have been using this tangy sauce, and now it's available in selected grocery stores and by mail order.

EL PASO CHILE COMPANY
909 Texas Ave., El Paso, TX 79901. (915) 544-3434 or (800) 27-IS-HOT
This family-owned-and-operated company has been supplying folks across the country with specialty foods and spices for over 13 years. Drop in the store to meet cookbook author and co-owner Park Kerr and to look over the store's collection of sauces, marinades, and even chile linguini. By mail order, you can choose from salsas, jalapeño jelly, salsa mayonnaise, and Mexican specialty ingredients such as mole paste, pickled serranos, pickled pequins, chipotle peppers, nopalitos, and ground habanero. Look for barbecue items like tequila barbecue sauce, beer barbecue sauce, and Holy Smoke Grilling Chips in hickory, mesquite, or fruitwood.

HILL COUNTRY FOODS
2933 Lady Bird Ln., Dallas, TX 75220. (214) 350-3370
Barbecue sauces and rubs from Hill Country Foods are available at grocery stores in Texas and by mail order. The dry rubs are Frank's 301 Barbecue Seasoning and the Hill Country Farms Mesquite Barbecue Seasoning. There's also the Across the Border Boogie Woogie BBQ Sauce, a dark rich sauce sold in an easy-to-pour jar.

JARDINE'S GENERAL STORE
Jardine Ranch, P.O. Box 160, Buda, TX 78610. (800) 544-1880

In Texas the name Jardine is synonymous with gourmet gift food. If it can be bottled or boxed and it relates to Texas cuisine, it's probably in the Jardine catalog. Barbecue buffs will want to check out the 5-Star Bar-B-Q Sauce, Margarita Bar-B-Q Sauce, Mesquite Flavor Bar-B-Q Sauce, and, for the really brave, the Killer Hot Bar-B-Q Sauce. If you swing through Buda (located just south of Austin on I-35), stop by for a look around the factory.

KING'S ROUGE
P.O. Box 164163, Austin, TX 78716-4163. (No phone orders.)

This tomato-based sauce is a blend of sugars, vegetables, and fruits, a mixture that proclaims itself "A Sauce for All Occasions." It's all natural and fat free, a peppery blend that does not include smoke flavoring, relying instead on the flavor you've imparted to the meat in your smoker.

LIENDO PLANTATION
618 10th St., P.O. Box 454, Hempstead, TX 77445. (800) 826-4371

The Liendo Plantation sells fajita marinade, pepper sauce, picante sauces, salsas, and Texas specialties like peach cobbler mix, pralines, and their Texas cow pattie fudge. Order by mail or visit the store an hour northwest of Houston. The Liendo Plantation was built in 1853 and was one of the state's first cotton plantations.

NEIMAN MARCUS
1618 Main St., Dallas, TX 75201. (800) 937-9146

For true Texas chic, shoppers head to Neiman Marcus and sauce buyers look for Red River, the brand of sauce this Dallas company has produced for over a decade. A Western-style kraft paper label brands these 16-ounce bottles, identifying a variety for every barbecue taste: beer, tequila, smokey, jalapeño, mesquite, hot, and hickory. If you just can't decide, go for the barbecue sauce sampler with five 8-ounce bottles for a taste of the products from the store that has been a Texas legend since 1907.

NEW CANAAN FARMS
P.O. Box 386, Dripping Springs, TX 78620. (800) 727-JAMS

New Canaan is sort of the Knotts Berry Farm of Texas, known for its delicious jams and jellies. These folks can turn on the spice, though, with their Texas Pride Barbeque Sauce and the Hickory Smoked Mustard. The farm is located on Highway 290, five miles west of Dripping Springs on a 10-acre site where Lyndon Baines Johnson gave his first political speech on July 4, 1930. Take a tour of the Hill Country Museum, look around a turn-of-the-century kitchen, walk the nature trails, and then shop while you enjoy free lemonade and cookies.

PACE FOODS INC.
P.O. Box 12636, San Antonio, TX 78212. (800) 433-PACE

Spice up your barbecue with this favorite Texas condiment, a concoction of jalapeño peppers, onions, and chiles. Call the toll-free number for order forms.

PITT'S & SPITT'S
14221 Eastex Fwy., Houston, TX 77032. (800) 521-2947

This pit manufacturer also makes seasonings and sauces, from a fajita and brisket marinade to steak seasoning and barbecue sauce.

ROYER'S ROUND TOP CAFE
On the Square, Round Top, TX 78954. (409) 249-3611

Order a bottle of pepper sauce from this excellent restaurant located on the square in Round Top. Like the bottles of vinegar and peppers found on the tables in Texas's best barbecue joints, this sauce will perk up any meat. It's a combination of peppers and cilantro suspended in vinegar, all sold in bottles ranging from small to magnum or in a heart-shaped gift bottle.

RUDY'S BARBECUE SAUCE
P.O. Box 691365, San Antonio, TX 78269. (210) 698-7177

Order up a few bottles of Rudy's unbeatable sauce, the same as served in the barbecue joint.

SOUTH TEXAS SPICE COMPANY
**P.O. Box 680086, San Antonio, TX 78268. (210) 684-6239
or fax (210) 684-7755**

Order some barbacoa or barbecue seasonings or some brisket seasoning with tenderizer from this spice and herb company. If you're looking for chile for your beans, you'll find 5 kinds of powder, 5 types of chile peppers, 11 varieties of pods, and 4 types of flakes on this mail order list.

SPECIALTY SAUCES
(800) SAUCES1 (728-2371)

This out-of-state company specializes in the barbecue sauces of the top pits in the country. Order up some of Sonny Bryan's sauce and see how it compares to the product of Arthur Bryant's Barbecue (Kansas City), McClard's Bar-B-Q

(Hot Springs, Arkansas), Charlie Robinson's #1 Rib Restaurant (Chicago), or John Wills Bar-B-Que Bar and Grill (Memphis).

STUBB'S LEGENDARY BAR-B-Q SAUCE
East Broadway Q Corporation, P.O. Box 4941, Austin, TX 78765.
(512) 480-0203

Christopher "Stubb" Stubblefield was an Austin 'que legend in the 1970s. The pitmaster opened a place that quickly became known not only for its meat but also its music. Performers like Joe Ely, Stevie Ray Vaughn, Muddy Waters, Willie Nelson, and Johnny Cash dropped in and "sang for their supper." Today Stubb has moved his pit to Lubbock and still serves terrific barbecue with a side order of live music. When you can't make it to Lubbock, though, you can still enjoy a taste of Stubb's with these original or spicy barbecue sauces. Stubb's also sells a dry rub, a vinegar-based marinade, chili fixings, serrano peppers, and two types of chowchow.

TRULY TEXAS BARBECUE SAUCE
J. B. Lags, Inc., P.O. Box 139, Georgetown, TX 78627-0139.
(512) 869-1977

This barbecue sauce calls itself Truly Texas, and it is just that. Made in and distributed from Georgetown, just north of Austin, the sauce is sold at over 200 gift shops in this country and as far away as France. It's made with tomato sauce, Worcestershire sauce, lemon juice, a touch of mesquite, and some other secret spices that make barbecue perk up. The sauce is available by mail order only to out-of-state customers. Texans will find it in the nine Truly Texas retail stores located in Killeen, Waco, Abilene, San Angelo, Odessa, Midland, Irving, Hurst, and Denton. The retail stores sell gourmet food products, mitts, aprons, and cookbooks, as well as Texas-shaped goodies of all varieties.

BARBECUED MEATS AND SAUSAGE

BODACIOUS BAR-B-Q
1450 Hwy. 377 E., P.O. Box 1980, Granbury, TX 76048. (817) 573-3921 or (800) 339-0279

Bodacious Bar-B-Q has some bodacious meats available by mail order: pork ribs, sausage, ham, beef, and turkey. This joint south of Fort Worth may be best known as the supplier of another barbecue delicacy—emu. Order smoked emu meat by the pound: The consistency is more like beef than poultry, and your order is carved off roasts barbecued much like red meat.

COUNTY LINE AIR RIBS
(800) 344-RIBS

You're trapped in New York, Boston, or some other uncivilized place devoid of good barbecue. You want ribs, and you want them now. Call County Line Air Ribs. Within 24 to 48 hours you'll have your choice of beef ribs, baby back pork ribs, sliced brisket, or sausage, arriving with enough barbecue sauce to brighten those "I'm not in Texas" blues. The meat is flash frozen and ready to reheat when you receive it. Shipped from the Colorado Springs County Line restaurant, the meat is prepared using the same recipes as found at the County Line headquarters in Austin.

GUADALUPE PIT SMOKED MEATS
1229 Gruene Rd., New Braunfels, TX 78130. (800) 880-0416

One night you're going to dream about barbecue, perfect barbecue, barbecue so tender you're ready to jump in the car and go the distance. Sit back and pick up the phone instead, especially if you're not in the vicinity of Gruene or San Antonio. (If you are, head to one of Guadalupe's restaurants; see the restaurant section for locations.) Dial the toll-free number and place your order for beef brisket, pork ribs, sausage, turkey breast, or the Guadalupe Barbecue sauce in original or hot. If only all dreams could come true as easily as this one.

NEW BRAUNFELS SMOKEHOUSE
P.O. Box 311159, New Braunfels, TX 78131-1159. (800) 537-6932

Select from hand-rubbed brisket smoked for 18 hours, summer sausage, bratwurst, pork ribs, and beef sausage, all slow-cooked over hickory. The Smokehouse also has a monthly gift plan so you can send someone really special (or yourself!) a taste of Texas every month.

OAKRIDGE SMOKEHOUSE GIFTS
P.O. Box 146, Schulenburg, TX 78956-0146. (800) 548-6325

Call and ask for a free catalog, then take your time selecting from these scrumptious selections. Smoked turkey, hams, pork chops, sausage, turkey and beef jerky, chicken, brisket, and sirloin tip are all tempting choices. This company is operated by the same family that owns the Oakridge Smokehouse Restaurant in Schulenburg (see the restaurant section).

ROBERTSON'S HAMS
I-35 exit 285, Salado, TX 76571. (800) 458-HAMS

Robertson's sells smoked ham, bacon, sausage, turkey, jerky, ribs, smoked cheese, and a dark barbecue sauce. The ham is rubbed with sugar cure and smoked over green hickory. Gift crates are also available.

BARBECUE PITS

KLOSE BAR-B-QUE PITS
2214-1/2 W. 34th St., Houston, TX 77018. (800) 487-PITS

This company has smokers in just about every size, from 24-inch-long models to huge trailered outfits that span 120 inches. Klose also caters and rents pits.

PITT'S & SPITT'S
14221 Eastex Fwy., Houston, TX 77032. (800) 521-2947

If it's barbecue related, then you name it and this place has got it. Pits, from a standard size to one mounted atop a trailer, stainless steel utensils, braziers, thermometers, knife sharpeners, broilers, injectors, camp stoves, cookbooks, and spices are all for sale in this general store of barbecue.

WOOD

JACOBS AND SON ENTERPRISES, INC.
504 W. Pierce, San Saba, TX 76877. (915) 372-3298

Order mesquite and hickory wood chips or chunks and charcoal by the bag from this central Texas wholesaler and retailer.

APPENDIX C
BARBECUE ASSOCIATIONS AND PUBLICATIONS

ASSOCIATIONS

Barbecue clubs bring together pitmasters from around the state to swap news, share cook-off information, and just enjoy each other's company.

CENTRAL TEXAS BARBECUE ASSOCIATION
Rt. 5, 83 Helm
Temple, TX 76501
(817) 986-2694

EAST TEXAS BARBECUE COOKERS ASSOCIATION
2709 Cedarcrest
Marshall, TX 75670

INTERNATIONAL BARBECUE COOKERS ASSOCIATION
P.O. Box 300556
Arlington, TX 76007-0556

NATIONAL BARBECUE ASSOCIATION
P.O. Box 29051
Charlotte, NC 28229

NORTH TEXAS AREA BBQ COOKERS ASSOCIATION
North Texas Fairgrounds
P.O. Box 3024
Denton, TX 76201

PUBLICATIONS

Some folks aren't happy just cooking or eating barbecue; they like to spend their time away from the pit reading about their barbecue buddies. Keep up with the cook-offs, the latest products, and the folks that make the barbecue world go 'round with these publications, or contact the various associations listed above about receiving their newsletters.

THE PITS

7714 Hilliard, Dallas, TX 75217. (214) 747-5537

This tabloid, published monthly March through December, looks at barbecue around Texas and surrounding states, offering results of recent cook-offs and announcements of upcoming ones.

GOAT GAP GAZETTE

5110 Baynard Ln. #2, Houston, TX 77006. (713) 523-2362

This tabloid calls itself the "Clarion of the Chili World," but it also has plenty of information for barbecue buffs. Published 11 times a year, the paper includes listings of upcoming barbecue cook-offs in Texas and neighboring states—even some as far away as Canada.